Agustín de Salazar y Torres
Juan de Vera Tassis y Villarroel
Sor Juana Inés de la Cruz

EL ENCANTO ES LA HERMOSURA Y EL HECHIZO SIN HECHIZO
LA SEGUNDA CELESTINA

MEDIEVAL & RENAISSANCE

TEXTS & STUDIES

VOLUME 128

Agustín de Salazar y Torres
Juan de Vera Tassis y Villarroel
Sor Juana Inés de la Cruz

EL ENCANTO ES LA HERMOSURA Y EL HECHIZO SIN HECHIZO LA SEGUNDA CELESTINA

(*BEAUTY IS ENCHANTING AND BEWITCHMENT WITHOUT WITCHCRAFT*) (*THE SECOND CELESTINA*)

Critical Edition, Introduction, and Notes by

THOMAS AUSTIN O'CONNOR

Medieval & Renaissance texts & studies
Binghamton, New York
1994

A grant from The Program for Cultural Cooperation Between
Spain's Minisitry of Culture and United States' Universities
has helped meet publication costs of this book.

Library of Congress Cataloging-in-Publication Data

Salazar y Torres, Agustín, 1642–1675.
[Encanto es la hermosura y el hechizo sin hechizo]
El encanto es la hermosura y el hechizo sin hechizo (La segunda Celestina) = Beauty is enchanting and bewitchment without witchcraft (The second Celestina) / Agustín de Salazar y Torres, Juan de Vera Tassis y Villarroel, sor Juana Inés de la Cruz ; critical edition, introduction, and notes by Thomas Austin O'Connor.
p. cm. — (Medieval & Renaissance texts & studies)
Includes the two conclusions to Salazar y Torres' unfinished play, the first by Juan de Vera Tassis y Villarroel, and the second attributed to Sister Juana Inés de la Cruz.
Includes bibliographical references.
ISBN 0–86698–135–7
1. Salazar y Torres, Agustín, 1642–1675. Encanto es la hermosura y el hechizo sin hechizo. I. Vera Tassis y Villarroel, Juan de, 17th/18th cent. II. Juana Inés de la Cruz, Sister, 1651–1695. III. O'Connor, Thomas Austin, 1943– . IV. Title. V. Title: Beauty is enchanting and bewitchment without witchcraft (The second Celestina). VI. Title: Segunda Celestina. VII. Title: 2. Celestina. VIII. Title: Second Celestina. IX. Title: 2nd Celestina. X. Series.
PQ6431.S24E6 1994b
862–dc20 94–39557
CIP

This book is made to last.
It is set in Bembo
and printed on acid-free paper
to library specifications

Printed in the United States of America

Table of Contents

For Don Gonzalo Torrente Ballester,

My Friend and Mentor:

A grateful mind
By owing owes not, but still pays, at once
Indebted and discharg'd.
Milton: *Paradise Lost*

CYTHARA DE APOLO,

LOAS, Y COMEDIAS DIFERENTES

QVE ESCRIVIÓ
D. AGVSTIN DE SALAZAR Y TORRES;
Y SACA A LVZ
D. IVAN DE VERA TASIS Y VILLARROEL,
SV MAYOR AMIGO;
OFRECIENDOLAS
A LA CATHOLICA MAGESTAD
DE
DOÑA MARIANA DE AVSTRIA Nª. Sª
AVGVSTA REINA MADRE,
POR MANO
DEL EXCELENTISSIMO SEÑOR
D. ANTONIO SEBASTIAN DE TOLEDO,
MARQVES DE MANCERA,
Señor de las Cinco Villas, &c.

SEGVNDA PARTE.

CON PRIVILEGIO.

EN MADRID: A costa de *Francisco Sanz*, Impressor del Reyno, y Portero de Camara de su Magestad. Año 1681.
Vendese en su Imprenta, en la Plazuela de la Calle de la Paz.

Preface

In 1990 Guillermo Schmidhuber de la Mora published in Mexico an edition of *La segunda Celestina* (The second Celestina) in which he attributed to Sor Juana Inés de la Cruz the conclusion of, and "una colaboración generosa en" (a generous collaboration in [Sor Juana de la Cruz 1990, 11]), an unfinished play by the Hispano-Mexican poet and dramatist, Agustín de Salazar y Torres (1642–1675). Until fairly recently, the ending of *La segunda Celestina* was considered anonymous by bibliographers and theater specialists of Spain's Golden Age (1580–1700). A better-known version of the work, titled *El encanto es la hermosura y el hechizo sin hechizo* (Beauty is enchanting and bewitchment without witchcraft), contains a conclusion written by Don Juan de Vera Tassis y Villarroel, the editor of Salazar's complete works. The publication of Schmidhuber's edition, with its hypothesis concerning Sor Juana's authorship, produced an immediate polemical reaction in Mexican criticism. The present edition will not resolve all the questions stirred up by that polemic; however, it should provide to interested parties a textual and critical base from which to examine them with a scientific objectivity that is assuredly highly desirous, but difficult (if not impossible) to realize in practice.

The present edition includes the two conclusions to Salazar's unfinished play and a brief discussion of some of the relevant themes: authorship of the distinct finales; dating of each theatrical premiere and of the first editions; dramatic nature of the part written by Salazar and agreement of the distinct endings with the plan envisioned by him; and, finally, three appendices that supply variants from the early editions. Appendix 1 provides some clues to Vera Tassis's editorial practices and habits, for, in the idiom of the period, he "emended and corrected" Salazar's original manuscript.

Although the Salazarian text may appear at first glance to be a typical cape-and-sword play (*comedia de capa y espada*) that follows the model established by Don Pedro Calderón de la Barca (1600–1681), in truth it is a hybrid creation that seeks to harmonize elements from two distinct *Comedia* genres: *la comedia de capa y espada* and the play of magic (*la comedia de magia*). The dual title of the version completed by Vera

Tassis underscores this generic hybridism. This point will prove decisive in examining and evaluating the two endings, because Vera Tassis emphasized the magic potential of the text left by Salazar, whereas Sor Juana stressed characteristic elements of the play of intrigue (*la comedia de intriga*) common at that time.

The texts we have inherited from these three dramatists remind us of a self-evident historical and theatrical fact, one which is perhaps difficult for us to accommodate easily in our present historical consciousness: in the seventeenth century there was a common dramatic tradition in the cultural community of Spanish-speaking peoples. *El encanto es la hermosura y el hechizo sin hechizo,* a play first performed in Madrid in 1675 or 1676 for the Spanish court, was quickly staged in the Coliseum of New Spain (Mexico), probably in 1679. A little later, but before the production of Sor Juana's *Los empeños de una casa* (One house's involvements) in 1683, a version of the former play entitled *La Celestina* was put on stage in Mexico City, with an ending most likely written by her. The facts dealing with the composition, production, and transmission of the texts which are currently available to us are few, and they fail to answer satisfactorily all the questions that have proven to be troublesome. Nevertheless, in the same spirit of critical openness enunciated by Guillermo Schmidhuber in his prologue to *La segunda Celestina,* I also "pretend[o] iniciar una indagación crítica" (seek to initiate a critical inquiry) into this valuable composite text.

Finally, I would like to take this opportunity to thank the two outside reviewers, and my friend and colleague, Professor Salvador J. Fajardo, for their careful review of the original manuscript and many helpful suggestions. A special thanks is also owed to my wife Rae Carolyn for her inestimable and constant assistance in the preparation of this edition. I am indebted to Catherine Di Cesare, my MRTS editor, for invaluable assistance, particularly with the English version of the Introduction.

I close by sharing the sentiment expressed in the famous opening line of the "Prologue" to *Don Quixote,* I: "Idle Reader: Without any oath you may believe me that I would wish that this book, as the child of reason, were the most beautiful, the most elegant, and most discreet that could be imagined."

Vestal, New York
January 1994

Introduction

BIOGRAPHY OF DON AGUSTIN DE SALAZAR Y TORRES[1]

Don Agustín was born in Almazán (Soria)[2] on 28 August 1642 to Don Juan de Salazar y Bolea and Doña Petronila de Torres y Montalvo. At the age of five he went to New Spain (Mexico) with his maternal uncle, Don Marcos de Torres, Collegiate of the Major College of Santa Cruz de Valladolid and bishop of Campeche, Mexico, who died there while serving as viceroy. In his youth, Salazar studied the Greek, Latin, Italian, and Spanish poets, as well as the Humanities at the University of Mexico. Vera Tassis narrates an anecdote in which Salazar, before his twelfth birthday, recited the *Soledades* (Solitudes) and the *Polifemo* (Polyphemus) of Góngora from memory to the students and professors gathered in the College of the Company of Jesus, accompanied by the explication of their difficulties and obscure passages. In adolescence he excelled in courses dealing with arts and letters, canon law, theology, and astrology. He would put this knowledge to good use in his poetic and dramatic works, as may be seen in the ridicule of false astrology in *El encanto.*

In Mexico the young Salazar y Torres met Don Francisco Fernández de la Cueva, duque of Alburquerque, who had become viceroy and captain general of Mexico and served in that capacity from 1654 to 1660. To celebrate the arrival of this great nobleman to New Spain, Salazar wrote his "Descripción de la entrada pública en México del . . .

---

[1] The unique source of this biography of Agustín de Salazar y Torres, as well as those previously published, is the "Discourse on the Life and Works of Don Agustín de Salazar," written by Vera Tassis and published in the preliminary pages of *Cítara de Apolo*, vol. 1. All quotations, unless otherwise indicated, come from this "Discourse." Brief biographies appear in *Poetas líricos de los siglos XVI y XVII*, vol.2, de Adolfo de Castro; *Dramáticos posteriores a Lope de Vega*, vol. 2, de Ramón de Mesonero Romanos; and *Catálogo bibliográfico y biográfico del teatro antiguo español, desde sus orígenes hasta medianos del siglo XVIII*, of Cayetano Alberto de la Barrera y Leirado.

[2] In his tribute to the memory of Calderón de la Barca, *Obelisco fúnebre* (Funereal obelisk), Gaspar Agustín de Lara made it clear that Don Agustín was born in the town of Almazán, and not in Soria, as Vera Tassis has stated.

Duque de Alburquerque" (Description of the public entry into Mexico of . . . the duke of Alburquerque), which was published in México in 1653. Perhaps this customary adulation of the proud nobleman led to the duke's continuing protection and constant assistance of the young writer. On the other hand, Salazar y Torres wrote *El amor más desgraciado, Céfalo y Pocris* (The most unfortunate love, Cephalus and Procris), possibly his best myth play, for the duke and duchess of Alburquerque.[3] He dedicated his "Fábula de Adonis y Venus" and other poems to the duchess, in addition to writing a prologue for Calderón's *Dar tiempo al tiempo* (Give time time), that was performed before the same noble couple. Another reminder of his stay in Mexico is "Los Metamorfoseos mexicanos" (The Mexican metamorphoses), in imitation of Ovid, that unfortunately has been lost. It is worth noting how lucky Salazar y Torres was to become acquainted with the duke of Alburquerque, a man known as "muy amigo de fiestas pomposas" (a good friend of sumptuous festivities).[4] The duke, who was very well placed at court—he bore the basin for the baptism of Carlos II,[5] in addition to occupying several important posts, such as being the chief steward (*mayordomo mayor*) of Carlos II in 1674 (Maura Gamazo 1911–1915, 2:210)—was the means by which the young Salazar y Torres presented himself to the Spanish court and entered its artistic and dramatic world.

Salazar y Torres returned to Spain in 1660 a protégé of the duke of Alburquerque, and probably in the same retinue of the intrepid nobleman. In Madrid his poetic talent was quickly recognized and praised. He imitated the dramatic style of Don Pedro Calderón de la Barca, particularly that utilized in royal festivities, and his plays were soon received with favor by the entire court, "empleándole los primeros señores della en las más célebres fiestas de sus reales majestades" (the important figures in it employing him in the most celebrated festivities of their royal majesties), as reported by Vera Tassis. The first known work of Salazar y Torres given at court was *Elegir al enemigo* (Choosing the enemy), performed on 6 November 1664, the third birthday of Don Carlos II. It was well received by courtiers and the general public alike, and at least thirteen editions of the play attest to its popularity and continuing theatrical success. A little after the brilliant launching of his career as a court dramatist, Salazar found himself without "empleo

---

[3] It was most likely produced during Shrovetide of 1667, 1668, or 1669 (O'Connor 1979).

[4] See the *Enciclopedia Espasa-Calpe* for the article on Don Francisco Fernández de la Cueva.

[5] See Maura Gamazo, 1911–15, 1: 57.

cortesano" (courtly employment), due to the death of Felipe IV on 17 September 1665; with the consequent prohibition of plays, the budding theatrical career of the young poet was interrupted.

During this first period at court, 1660–1666, Salazar y Torres married Doña Mariana Fernández de los Cobos, a native of Córdoba. After the wedding, Salazar travelled to Germany with the empress in the company of the duke of Alburquerque, recently appointed viceroy and captain general of Sicily, who served as mayordomo and leader of the party. The entourage of the infanta María Margarita left Spain on 28 April 1666 and arrived in Vienna, where the infanta met her husband Leopoldo I of Austria, on 5 December of the same year. After leaving Germany, Salazar occupied the post of sergeant major of the province of Agrigento (Girenti) in Sicily, and later the duke named him his Captain of Arms.

After the duke of Alburquerque had served for three years in the viceroyalty of Sicily, at the end of 1669 or the beginning of 1670, Salazar returned with him to Madrid in search of greater fortune. On his return to court, the writer entered into a very curious phase of his creative life. Vera Tassis relates that some ignorant courtiers, who did not recognize the poet's talent and failed to comprehend his art, envied his successes. On the other hand, Vera Tassis also states that intelligent courtiers admired Salazar and that the majority of the court loved him. In spite of his evident success in writing for royal festivities, Salazar continued to be a writer without good fortune, in terms of material wealth: "Fue tan gallarda su facundia, cuanto severa su desgracia" (His eloquence was as elegant as his misfortune severe).

Quickly the dramatist's talent once again made itself evident. The first known work presented to court in this period was *También se ama en el abismo* (There is also love in the abyss), most likely written for performance on 6 November 1670, the ninth birthday of Carlos II. There follows rapidly a series of mythic plays or works dealing with classical themes which were full of pomp, spectacle, music, and elegant verse. *Tetis y Peleo* (Thetis and Peleus) was probably performed for the first time on 22 December 1671, the birthday of the queen regent, Doña Mariana de Austria. There followed *Los juegos olímpicos* (The Olympic games) on 22 December 1673 and *El mérito es la corona y encantos de mar y amor* (Merit is the crown and enchantments of sea and love) in 1674 to celebrate the same royal festivity. All of these palace plays are most significant for the development of the Spanish *zarzuela,* a form partly declaimed and partly sung that deals, usually, with some mythological theme. Salazar was also an accomplished poet. For example, he imitated the *Soledades* of Góngora in "Las cuatro estaciones del día" (The four periods of the day), but the fourth, that of the night, was completed by Vera Tassis, who also wrote the ending to *El encanto es la hermosura.* Vera Tassis characterizes Salazar as a musical poet, whose "versos [son] los más suaves para el oído" (verses [are] most sweet to the ear).

Agustín de Salazar y Torres died in Madrid on 29 November 1675, weakened and atrophic from a grave and long illness that, fortunately, did not affect his reason. In 1681 Vera Tassis published the *Cítara de Apolo,* whose two volumes contain almost all the extant poetic and dramatic works of the talented *novohispano* writer.[6]

THE SPANISH CAPE-AND-SWORD PLAY

Although today we may be accustomed to viewing the production of plays from Spain's Golden Age according to a modern theatrical rhythm, with one intermission or without intermission between acts, such an aesthetic and theatrical practice does not conform to the fashion of that bygone age, in which the spectacle consisted of the presentation of a play accompanied by smaller dramatic and musical works called prologues (*loas*), one-act farces (*entremeses*), and dances (*bailes*). Throughout the seventeenth century there was constant criticism of the spectacle's dependence upon a love intrigue in the play and a coarse, even licentious humor in the accompanying pieces. Despite the criticism, this combination created a strong appeal for all social classes and led to a commercial success that assured the survival of this theatrical amalgam until the end of the eighteenth century.

In his famous and unusual "Aprobación" (Approbation) of the *Verdadera quinta parte de comedias* (True fifth part of plays) of Pedro Calderón de la Barca, Fray Manuel de Guerra y Ribera enumerated three classes of play in Calderón's dramatic oeuvre: 1) the saint play; 2) the play dealing with history; and 3) the amatory, or cape-and-sword, play. Recently Marc Vitse characterized the dominant dramatic works of the second half of the seventeenth century in a similar manner: 1) the myth play; 2) the heroic play; and 3) the cape-and-sword play (Vitse 1988, 135). In spite of the subgenres or taxonomy chosen, all Spanish plays presented to a greater or lesser degree a love intrigue as an essential ele-

---

[6] For information on the life and works of Vera Tassis, see La Barrera and Cruickshank. For the same on Sor Juana, see La Barrera. There are many studies dealing with Sor Juana, among which Octavio Paz's *Sor Juana o las trampas de la fe* warrants special mention.

ment in each plot. Reacting violently against Guerra's approbation of Spanish plays in 1682, the Jesuit P. Pedro Fomperosa y Quintana asserted in the following year that even the saint plays, accompanied by their *sainete* or *entremés* (one-act farces), did not free themselves from the omnipresent Spanish obsession with carnal love, exclaiming: "¿Qué junta es esta de afectos, de penitencias y liviandades?" (What kind of a union is this of emotion, penance, and licentiousness? [Cotarelo 1904, 265b]).

The Spanish cape-and-sword play definitively summarizes, in a pristine fashion, the allure of the entire *Comedia* genre, in which the power and mystery of human love are presented in their various facets as the axis of dramatic interest: courting / wooing, falling in love, jealousy, and, finally, marriage.[7]

Marc Vitse has observed that the Spanish *Comedia* endeavors to be a *speculum mundi, re-praesentatio totius naturae* (a mirror of the world, a representation of all nature [Vitse 1988, 257]). But that mirror distorts historic reality and its Spanish environment by idealizing, on the one hand, the conduct of some personages and by ridiculing, on the other, that of the comic figures. Spanish theater tends to create and present the dramatic world as prescribed by its respective genre, and not at all as it truly was. As Vitse has noted, the strong sense of decorum among Spaniards prevails in the theater over its other dramatic doctrine, verisimilitude.

In the cape-and-sword play, in particular, comedic exigencies affect all the characters, in order to provoke laughter from the audience. Nevertheless, the dramatic interest of the subgenre cape-and-sword play is based fundamentally on the physical, sexual, and personal attraction of two young people in the throes of the power, delirium, contradiction, torment, and ecstasy of heterosexual love. The amatory plays

---

[7] From the 1960s to the present, dramatic criticism of the cape-and-sword play has been appropriately evaluating and revising the theoretical bases of this famous, popular class of Comedia. The essays and studies by Honig, Mujica, ter Horst, Varey, Valbuena Briones, and Wardropper, cited in the Bibliography, initiated the process and continue to be the indispensable guide for its elucidation. The recent studies by Larson, Martino Crocetti, and Hildner make clear that critical interest in the subject has not abated. The paradigmatic plays that served and continue to serve as the focal point for the reevaluation are Calderón's *La dama duende* (The Phantom Lady) and *Casa con dos puertas mala es de guardar* (A house with two doors is difficult to guard). In general, critics insist on the fact that the cape-and-sword play is not merely a superficial entertainment, but a form that contains, or may contain, a serious purpose that communicates, through its individual dramatic world, a perception and appreciation of the human condition.

dramatize, without doubt, what anthropologists, ethnologists, biologists, and contemporary theater critics would characterize as a rite of courtship and falling in love that eventually leads, offstage, to the socially sanctioned mating of two young people.[8] Some commentators of the seventeenth and eighteenth centuries preferred to ignore this human reality or were unable to abide any representation of it that would suggest an implicit or explicit approval of the sensual or sexual pleasure that might accompany it.[9] The amatory plays, with their rites of courtship, created a natural and wholesome venereal sense in their spectators that instinctively confirmed the goodness of creation and the salubrity of their participation in natural processes.

In 1648 the Royal Council of Castile issued an opinion to the effect that the *Comedia* was directed at interests very different from those of "las comunidades pequeñas y asidas á la estrecheza y profesión religiosa" (small communities dedicated to austerity and religious profession) and instead found in the *Comedia* an exemplary morality for the lay estate, since it "[p]ropone los indultos castigados, y cuando más se extiende á lo profano finje los afectos amorosos reducidos á los límites del decoro que se encaminan y paran en los decentes fines del matrimonio" (proposes the punishment of excesses, and, when it most extends to the profane, it feigns amorous emotions subjected to the limits of decorum that are directed toward and transformed into the decent purposes of matrimony [Cotarelo 1904, 167a]). Not everyone shared this judgment, as evidenced by the commentary written in 1680 by Francisco Gutiérrez de los Ríos. According to him, the cape-and-sword play threatened social order and undermined traditional authority by presenting illicit love affairs (*amoríos*) that the eventual marriages only dissemble: "con el

---

[8] Early European theater originally associated comedy with fertility rites and the celebration of fecundity.

[9] Michel Foucault has observed that the "repressive hypothesis" concerning the open discussion of sexuality from the seventeenth century to the present distorts and misrepresents what in fact took place in discourse surrounding the issue. In this manner, the commentators referred to here were correct in criticizing what Foucault has called "la 'misc en discours' du sexe" (the "putting into discourse" of sex), but also bear some responsibility for its being placed there. Foucault states clearly that "What is at issue, briefly, is the over-all 'discursive fact,' the way in which sex is 'put into discourse.' Hence, too, my main concern will be to locate the forms of power, the channels it takes, and the discourses it permeates in order to reach the most tenuous and individual modes of behavior, the paths that give it access to the rare or scarcely perceivable forms of desire, how it penetrates and controls everyday pleasure—all this entailing effects that may be those of refusal, blockage, and invalidation, but also incitement and intensification: in short, the 'polymorphous techniques of power' " (Foucault 1990, 1: 11).

justo título de matrimonio se encubren los desordenados lances de amor ilícito" (with the just-in-time title of matrimony the disordered affairs of illicit love are concealed [Vitse 1988, 137]). Depending on the attitude assumed in confronting the phenomenon of human love and its theatrical representation, intellectuals and social and moral commentators, lay as well as clerical, expressed opinions that were at times hostile and frequently contradictory concerning theater in general and the cape-and-sword play in particular.

GREEK MYTH, SPANISH SOCIETY, AND THE ORDER OF NATURE: THE ROLE OF THE *PARTHENOS* / *DONCELLA* / MAIDEN IN THE CAPE-AND-SWORD PLAY

In her analysis of Greek myth, Barbara Smith contends that the Greek concept of *parthenos* "articulated the physical and conceptual space between [the] father's household/hearth and that of the husband. In other words, the *parthenos* was in between male-identified statuses" (Smith 1992, 87). The Spanish cape-and-sword play utilizes the in-between status of its female protagonists as the springboard for dramatic action. The *parthenos* (she who has begun menstruating) in her state as a *kore* (young woman or adolescent) represents the unmarried woman or Spanish maiden (*doncella*) who lives in her father's, brother's, or uncle's house, but who is destined to be the *gune* (wife or spouse) of a man of some other family. This social relationship cloaks the biological foundation of the *kore* as a virgin or maiden whose instrumental function is to eventually become a *meter* or mother. The Spanish cape-and-sword play ritually dramatizes this same transitional state which had served as the principal focus of many ancient Greek myths. Moreover, Smith classifies this state in ancient Greek society as an ambivalent sociopathological condition that requires treatment, in fact, a cure. As one finds amply verified in myth, there are only two social options for the Greek *parthenos:* transformation of the *kore* to *gune* and *meter,* or destruction.[10] To the Greek options, the Spanish *Comedia* added the possibility of entering a convent (perhaps, in social and biological terms, a variant of the second).

Barbara Smith emphasizes from a feminist perspective that the ambivalence of the ancient Greek male originated in a potentially

---

[10] The myth of Daphne, for example, communicates a system of values determined by the patriarchy, in spite of the importance given to the female personage and her disdain for the god Apollo.

threatening situation, one in which women could possibly escape from masculine control. According to David Adams Leeming, the Homeric and Olympian religion intended to defeminize the Great Goddess of antiquity by underscoring the virginity and the masculine aspect of figures such as Artemis and Pallas Athena (Leeming 1990, 109). Greek patriarchy conceptualized woman either as Athena, a symbol and representative of masculine values, or as Aphrodite, "whose exaggerated sexuality and stereotypical femininity is equally revealing of that system" (104). The Spanish *Comedia* addresses many of the same masculine concerns that serve as a basis for both Greek and European mythology.

On the first plane of dramatic action, Spanish *doncellas* and *damas* (maidens and ladies), equivalents of the Greek *parthenoi,* threaten social stability defined and defended, generally, by mature males. The fragility of familial honor (*honra*) demands that duennas and squires guard the maidens and that there be absolutely no contact with young noblemen. In fact, the threat that fathers experience comes both from those hard-to-control adolescent women and from those rambunctious young men who do not yet behave according to the social and class obligations established by tradition. The conflict is, in effect, intergenerational. Therefore, the cape-and-sword play frequently dramatizes the efforts expended by the older generation in attempting to control the energy and spontaneity of the *parthenoi* through arranged marriages, whose criteria do not necessarily correspond to their sentimental and emotional needs. Nevertheless, the action on the first plane, the intent to control the *parthenoi,* may mask another intent on the second that has much to do with the young men. The young nobleman, appearing free, is also seeking to marry his beloved or is seeking to escape from prior commitments made by his elders. In the meantime, the young maidens are transforming themselves, little by little and in secret, into wives, and the young men, into husbands. In the denouement of the intrigue, the young noblemen, in extending their hands to their beloveds, implicitly adopt the Spanish code of honor and begin at that moment to assume their responsibilities as future *paterfamilias*. On the surface, the young people have overcome all obstacles and vanquished the older generation. But society, in fact, comes out the winner, because in the long run the concluding marriage confirms societal norms and fulfills nature's designs. The matrimonial pledge, which now unites a young man and young woman, binding them both more tightly to the obligations of honor, underscores, according to Smith, "that *parthenos* had a temporal limitation and a finite social usefulness in its own right" (88). Although the onus and social impact of marriage seem to fall squarely on the hard-to-control *parthenoi,* the play's action slyly reminds the audience that the often rake-like young noblemen will, in turn, be brought to heel by similar societal and familial obligations. It's all a question of time.[11]

The cape-and-sword play defends the right of the young to choose a spouse, firmly rejecting one traditional principle of patriarchy, the absolute authority of the father in matrimonial matters.[12] On the other hand, we spectators witness more than the defense of personal liberty, because the play dramatizes at the same time a rite of socialization of two young people and their union as a conjugal couple, which will assure the continuation of the human species.[13]

For two centuries the cape-and-sword play provoked an intense and, at times, bitter debate due to the fact that it affirmed an essential and natural goodness in living and enjoying life, a position that Christian tradition had divorced from its conceptually questionable theological formulations of the purpose of human existence. The theatrical representation of sensual pleasure that arises from a broad spectrum of sexual relations put in doubt the question of the natural order that theologians, especially since the time of St. Augustine, had defined doctrinally. Once this natural order was defined, its estimation as irreparably corrupt determined, or should have determined (forever, according to some) social and moral practices and policies, in spite of the changing and evolving consciousness of human reality and potential that the Renaissance brought to Europe.

Even in 1675/1676 intellectuals, moralists, and other grave persons had not resolved the problems surrounding the cape-and-sword play. It is worth remembering that, according to the theoretician El Pinciano, "en la tragedia se enseña la vida que se debe huir, y en la comedia la que se debe seguir" (tragedy points out the life to be fled from, and comedy that to be followed [Vitse 1988, 323]). Many questioned what vital lessons young people, both unmarried youths and maidens, learned from the Spanish *Comedia*. Some responded without equivocation: Spanish plays are essentially (*per se*) lascivious, due to their dramatic material, since they present indecent models, *cosas torpes* (obscene affairs)

[11] The imposition of marriage as a restraint or bridle of young men's passions assists us in understanding King Alfonso's ongoing efforts to marry off Don Juan and Duke Octavio of *El burlador de Sevilla* (*The Mocker of Seville*).

[12] Paternal authority was based, according to Roman tradition, on the concept of *patria potestas*, the father's absolute control over the lives of his children.

[13] This outline does little justice to the essentially problematic nature of the formula that contemporary criticism is only now addressing, nor does it suggest the flexibility of its deployment in thousands of conflictive plots.

in the vocabulary of the period, that ardent young men and impressionable women, immature and mature, married and single alike, emulate. The most pernicious lessons include: 1) a rebellion against paternal authority; 2) a rejection of traditional ecclesiastical teachings on sexual morality; 3) an affective liberation of youth, both maidens and young men, from social practices inherited from antiquity. In short, the *Comedia* teaches *malas costumbres* (evil mores or customs).[14] Among the most serious injuries that result from them, Fray Jerónimo de la Cruz enumerated in 1635 the following two: 1) "armar traiciones la muger casada á su marido" (the married woman prepares to betray her husband);[15] and 2) "[a] la doncella la incitan á que piense lo que no sabe y desee lo que no entiende" (they incite the young maiden to think about that of which she is ignorant and to desire that which she does not understand [Cotarelo 1904, 203a]).

In 1672, three years before Salazar wrote *El encanto,* the *Junta Superior* (High Council) recommended to Queen Mariana de Austria that she proscribe Spanish theater because "[e]s cierto que el sugeto de que hoy se componen las comedias, son narraciones y fábulas amatorias" (it is certain that the subject matter of today's plays consists of amatory stories and fables [Cotarelo 1904, 388a]). And, two years after the production of *El encanto es la hermosura,* Don Francisco Ramos del Manzano, the preceptor of Carlos II and president of the Council of the Indies, confirmed once again the condemnation of cape-and-sword plays, since he found them "llenas de obscenidades" (rife with obscenities), and added: "y más aún los adherentes entremeses y bailes, que

---

[14] One should recall at this point that the criterion of "good" or "evil" customs or mores formed part of every ecclesiastical approbation, a requisite for the publication of any book or performance of any play. For example, in the approbation of *Cítara de Apolo* dated 20 January 1681, Pedro Calderón de la Barca wrote that he did not find in Salazar's works the slightest trace of anything "que repugne a la pureza de la fe y buenas costumbres" (that conflicts with the purity of faith and good mores" [¶¶7]).

[15] 1635 is the date of the most famous honor drama, Calderon's *El médico de su honra* (*The Surgeon of His Honor*), in which a husband suspects his wife's fidelity and love. Doña Mencía prepares apparent betrayals of Don Gutierre, who then feels obligated to kill her. The plot intrigues of comedies and tragedies have much in common. Thus, while in the cape-and-sword play what Barbara Smith describes as an ambivalent sociopathological condition in Greek myth, the "in between male-identified statuses" of the parthenoi, may be satisfactorily treated and cured by ritualized bonding or marriage, a symbolic "medical" intervention, in the wife-murder or honor dramas the cure demands an actual bloodletting or ritualized homicide. Doña Mencía's most serious error arises from a behavior more appropriate for a cape-and-sword play. See David Hildner's recent study.

ellos solos bastaban para hacer ilícitas las representaciones" (and more so the accompanying one-act farces and dances, for they alone would suffice to make their performance illicit [518a]). Despite Calderón's influence in making Spanish plays more decorous, an almost formulaic criticism was repeated at the close of the seventeenth century that owed much to that expressed at its beginning. In the *Primera parte de las excelencias de la virtud de la castidad* (On the excellencies of the virtue of chastity, part 1), published in 1601, the discalced Carmelite Fray José de Jesús María insisted that the *Comedia* was illicit: "Las comedias que se usan son indecentísimas y grandemente perjudiciales á todo género de gentes, porque muy pocas dejan de ser de *cosas lascivas y amores deshonestos*" (The plays that are performed are most indecent and gravely injurious to every class of people, because very few fail to be about *lascivious affairs and dishonest love affairs* [Cotarelo 1904, 370a; my emphasis]). To appreciate the hostile atmosphere toward creative activity, let the severity of the opinion of the important Jesuit P. Juan de Mariana that appeared in 1609 serve as example: according to him, theatrical pleasure (*deleite*) and literary enjoyment (*goce*) are identified with sinful acts (Mariana 1609).

As Marc Vitse has shown, the classification of theater's opponents and defenders into two groups, clerics the one and lay people the other, is a serious misreading of history. Fray Gaspar de Villarroel, an Augustinian preacher who eventually became bishop of Lima in 1659, was a conscientious clerical defender of Spanish theater. His criticism of the position of Doctor Don Juan Machado de Chaves, author of *Confesor perfecto* (The perfect confessor), provides some idea of the tone of the debate on theatrical licitness. Doctor Chaves had called the *Comedia's* dramatic material obscene or indecent (*torpe*), to which Fray Gaspar responded:

> Yo me persuado á que este autor y yo entendemos la palabra *torpe* con diversidad. El llama torpe todo lo amatorio, y ahí puede haber indiferencia, porque unos amores honestamente referidos no inducen á pecar juicios cuerdos . . . yo entiendo la palabra torpe cuando la uso . . . es pintar los amores torpemente; y en estas torpezas no tienen los poetas disculpa. (Cotarelo 1904, 600b)

> [I am convinced that this author and I understand the word *obscene* dissimilarly. He labels everything dealing with love as obscene, and there it is possible to have indifference (lack of importance), because some honestly narrated love affairs do not lead those of good judgment into sin. . . . I take the word obscene, when I use it . . . it means to depict love affairs in an obscene fashion; and in these obscenities poets have no excuse.]

This Augustinian defended the inherent goodness of human love and the lawfulness of its representation in the public theaters of Spain. And, what is even more significant, Fray Gaspar had confidence in the moral maturity of spectators and in their capacity to legitimately enjoy a theatrical entertainment that celebrated this love and the civil state to which it corresponded.

In the second half of the seventeenth century, the cape-and-sword play evinced unmistakable Calderonian influences, according to Fray Manuel de Guerra, Bances Candamo, and others, especially in the presentation of a love intrigue whose incidents were handled decorously by dramatists. Nevertheless, several critics interpreted even the word decorum dissimilarly, much as the word obscene (*torpe*) had different interpretations, as Fray Gaspar had observed. In 1660 Juan de Zabaleta considered the cape-and-sword plays indecorous in their ability to effect mores (*para hacer costumbres*), due to the fact that they "están hirviendo en afectos de amor" (are boiling with amorous affections [Vitse 1988, 309]). Eight years later Juan Caramuel, as Fray Gaspar before him, distinguished clearly between the dramatic material and the manner of its performance: "los amores narrados con castas y decentes palabras no se juzgan pertenecer a aquellas [comedias] cuyas representaciones inmediatamente deban prohibirse" (the love affairs narrated with chaste and decent words are not judged to pertain to those [plays] whose performance should be immediately prohibited [Vitse 1988, 215]). What, truly, did the cape-and-sword play teach to Spanish youth? According to some (though not all, as we have seen), that which is necessary to live well and prudently their lay estate.

In order to appreciate the unusual value of Fray Manuel de Guerra's approbation of 1682, a document of great importance for the history of theater in Spain, it is necessary to place it within the long and unfailingly positive tradition of ecclesiastical approbations which judged Spanish theater to be a decorous and appropriate entertainment for lay people. With a particularly acute historicist perspective, Guerra took great pains to explain in a detailed fashion why the Spanish *Comedia* is decorous and how it shares nothing in common with the reprehensible practices of classical Roman comedy, uniformly condemned by the fathers of the church. Moreover, Guerra made a proposition that created a veritable scandal, especially among some moralists and theologians, contending that "todas [las comedias] son tan ceñidas á las leyes de la modestia que no son peligro, sino doctrina" (all [plays] adhere so tightly to the laws of modesty that they present no danger, but rather doctrine [Cotarelo 1904, 334b]). According to Guerra, Calderón's plays represent on stage an idealization of deportment that transforms these works into a positive motivational force leading to correct and decent conduct. Addressing the cape-and-sword plays, Guerra wrote that "[s]i son de pasos amatorios (que son las menos morales) están tratados con tal honestidad, que ni se permite indecencia ligera en los afectos, ni voz menos pura que no saliese castigada a silvos" (if they deal with love scenes [for they are the least moral] they are handled with such propriety that the slightest indecency is not allowed in the emotions, or any suggestive word that is not rejected by whistling [334b]). In short, the Spanish *Comedia* is, according to Fray Manuel, modest and decent, and it teaches a doctrine appropriate to the lay estate with its conjugal responsibilities and rights.[16]

The debate over the lawfulness of Spanish theater quickly became entangled in political issues, especially those dealing with religious orders. The Jesuit P. Agustín de Herrera immediately answered Guerra, defending in passing his colleague and coreligionist P. Hurtado, who was impugned in Guerra's approbation. He employed a by-now traditional criticism that Fray José de Jesús María alleged in 1601, without taking into account the substantial plot changes and formal modifications brought about by Calderón: "En fin, todo es un amor que, mudado el nombre, en la realidad es lascivia" (In short, it is all a love that, with a change of name, is really lasciviousness [355a]). P. Herrera explains very clearly his position, which is shared by others, and reveals that he fears the effect of the *Comedia,* because it will take away "insensiblemente el horror cristiano y honrado á la culpa del amor lascivo, de suerte que no espante como torpe, sino que alhague y lisonjee como honroso, bizarro y entendido" (imperceptibly the Christian and honorable horror from the guilt of lascivious love, so that it may not frighten as obscene, but rather flatter and delight as proper, gallant, and sophisticated [356a]). In other words, the Spanish *Comedia,* with its portrayal of the inherent goodness of human love, challenges a theological and doctrinal tradition that the Christian community inherited from the fathers of the church, in particular from St. Augustine, and that progressively gained strength from the Middle Ages onward. For this reason, Guerra's assertion that the *Comedia* teaches a doctrine for lay people received the following response from Herrera: "Doctrina en que

[16] It is possible that some readers, particularly some specialists in Golden Age theater, may view the theme of theatrical licitness as more suitable to a type of dramatic criticism of a moral bent now out of fashion. My purpose is different, since I wish to focus on the theme of licitness as an example of the conflict that results from the slow and inevitable secularization that Spanish society underwent in the seventeenth century.

se enseña á los galanes, todos los medios de obligar á las damas y á las damas el modo de corresponder á los galanes" (A doctrine in which lovers are shown all manner of obligating their ladies and ladies the way to repay their beaux [356a]). This astute Jesuit demonstrated in this short phrase that he clearly understood the basic rule and ritualized dynamic of the cape-and-sword play and its allure for the public.

Marc Vitse's study of *El hombre práctico* (The practical man), written by the theatrical reformer Gutiérrez de los Ríos in 1680, summarizes the criticism of the *Comedia* by both lay and clerical opponents and reformers according to three criteria: 1) a timeless sexual morality; 2) a familial morality; and 3) a social morality (135). Although theologians would be principally concerned with the first criterion, the serious men of the seventeenth century also addressed the last two. Another Jesuit, P. Pedro Fomperosa y Quintana, became interested in the *Comedia* and, in passing, demonstrated an understanding of it that would come to characterize the following century:

> Muchas de las comedias amatorias modernas contienen doctrinas que enseñan modos de pecar, solicitar doncellas por medios ilícitos, papeles, sobornos, tercerías, etc., venganzas y otras libertades, y algunas de ellas deshonestidades sobradamente claras en el verso, pinturas de mujeres desnudas, acciones livianas de abrazarse, tomarse las manos, y otras monerías amatorias de los sainetes, con mucho mayor peligro en los pocos años de perder la castidad á vista de la hermosura desenvuelta de aquellas mujeres, y otras muchas ocasiones que llevan los teatros. (Cotarelo 1904, 264b)

> [Many of the modern amatory plays contain doctrines that instruct in the ways of sin, how to court maidens with illicit means, notes, bribes, go-betweens, etc., revenge and other liberties, and some of them (plays) all too clear obscenities in the verses, depictions of nude women, lewd actions such as embracing, grasping each other's hands, and other amusing love tricks of the farces, with much greater danger for the young of losing their chastity in the presence of the dissolute beauty of those women (actresses), and many other occasions (of sin) that theaters create.][17]

---

[17] *Fineza contra fineza* (Courtesy matched by courtesy) was performed in Vienna on 22 December 1671, the birthday of Queen Mariana of Austria, and published in Calderón's *Cuarta parte* (Fourth part). In the work, Anfión, son of the mythic Acteón, describes what occurred to his father in this way:

conque corrida de verse
vista Diana; bien como

Discounting the unrestrained exaggeration, one finds a description of many of the dramatic situations in *El encanto es la hermosura* and *La segunda Celestina*.

Some commentators from the second half of the seventeenth century had developed their sense of decorum to such an extent that, for them, every amatory expression would inevitably lead to some obscenity, and the cape-and-sword play, in particular, would encourage evil behavior. In an anonymous letter taking issue with P. Guerra's approbation, the author characterized the *Comedia* as a "staged *Arte amandi*" and cited *La segunda Celestina* as the evil employment of a go-between in plays (Vitse 1988, 152).[18] Nevertheless, at the same time as Guerra defended the exemplary doctrine of the decorous and decent play based on the Calderonian model, so too did Bances Candamo, in his *Teatro de los teatros* (The theater of theaters), emphasize that "todo el discurso de la comedia puede ser escuela de los buenos casados y al fin terror de los malos" (all the discourse of the *Comedia* can be a school for good spouses and eventually a horror for bad ones [Cotarelo 1904, 78b]). The couples at the conclusions of *El encanto es la hermosura* and *La segunda Celestina* stand as examples of the first, and for the second one

---

a la verdad pintar suelen,
por no dezir que desnuda;
tanto su desdoro siente,
que afuer de casta deidad
se vengó; como si fuesse
delito el acaso; en fin
que no quiero detenerme
en retoricas pinturas,
que peligra lo decente
donde ay baños, y beldades. (Calderón 1672, 522a)

[So, when Diana became ashamed of discovering herself observed; well, as they are accustomed to portraying it all, in order not to say in the nude; so much did she feel this blot (on her reputation), that, as a chaste deity, she avenged herself; as if chance were a crime; in short, I do not want to tarry in rhetorical descriptions, for decency is in danger when beauties attend to their baths.]

The modern edition, by Valbuena Briones, has "indecoro" (impropriety) instead of "desdoro" (blemish or stain) of the original. Evidently Calderón pokes fun at the fastidious sensibilities of some of his contemporaries by saying it without saying it, and such textual evidence from a court play clearly demonstrates that the theme of decorum and that of "nudity" were keenly felt at that time.

[18] This letter, written in 1682, contains the earliest mention of *La segunda Celestina* that I am aware of, and I suspect that *El encanto es la hermosura* was also referred to in Spain by this popular title. This newly-discovered information affects my discussion of the title *La "segunda" Celestina* in *Literatura Mexicana* (O'Connor 1992, 294) and, therefore, has led to its revision here.

has only to refer to any Calderonian wife-murder drama, such as *El médico de su honra*.

In 1690 Bances examined very carefully the Calderonian cape-and-sword play and described it thus:

> El argumento de ésta, por mayor parte, se reduce al galanteo de una mujer noble con una cortesana competencia de otro amante, con varios duelos entre los dos ó más por los términos decentes de la cortesanía, que pára en casarse con ella el uno después de muy satisfecho de su honor y de que no favoreció á los otros, y en desengañarse los demás. (Cotarelo 1904, 77b–78a)

> [Its plot, in the main, is boiled down to the wooing of a noble woman with courtly competition from another suitor, with various duels between the two or more based on the decent terms of courtesy, that ends in the one marrying her after being very satisfied about her honor and that she never favored the others, and with the disillusionment of all others.]

A hundred years later the same theme was being discussed, and with the same vehemence. Gaspar Melchor de Jovellanos summarized more than two hundred years of debate on theatrical lawfulness with these almost exasperated words:

> El problema parece indeciso aun en nuestros días y mientras el gobierno se convierte á mejorar y perfeccionar los espectáculos, hay gentes que se atreven todavía á predicar y escribir que es un grave pecado autorizarlos, consentirlos y concurrir á ellos. (Cotarelo 1904, 385b)

> [The problem appears undecided even in our days, and while the government directs itself to bettering and improving (public) spectacles, there are people who still dare to preach and write that it is a grave sin to authorize them, to permit them, and to attend them.]

There was no alternative, according to Jovellanos, because it was now necessary "reformarle [el teatro] ó proscribirle para siempre" (to reform it [the theater] or proscribe it forever [386a]). Cotarelo comments on Jovellanos's proposal, to exclude from the theater the emotion of human love, concluding that it would result in exiling from it its very soul (386b–87a). Jovellanos supported the docent function of theater. At the same time he preferred, as a typical eighteenth-century intellectual, to limit its lessons to the fostering of good civic behavior, notwithstanding the fact that amatory feelings were not obscene and did not necessarily lead to lascivious love affairs. The well-reasoned position of the Council of Castile in 1648, that the *Comedia* feigns "los afectos amorosos reducidos á los límites del decoro que se encaminan y paran en los decentes fines del matrimonio" (amatory emotions subjected to the limits of decorum that are directed toward and transformed into the decent purposes of matrimony [167a]), never could persuade those who did not appreciate or even looked down on matrimony as a legitimate state for the human being.[19]

THE SOCIAL CODES AND PLOT CONVENTIONS OF THE CAPE-AND-SWORD PLAY

As P. Agustín de Herrera indicated, the cape-and-sword play functions according to a code of love that governs the conduct of each noble person. The gallant seeks to obligate (*obligar*) his beloved, and the lady, once obligated, then must find some way to repay (*corresponder*) her beau. This amatory code either operates in tandem with, or in opposition to, the more famous *código del honor* (code of honor). In *El encanto* a very clear distinction is established between nobles who act or should act in accordance with values idealized by the codes of love and

[19] Contemporary criticism of Golden Age theater was greatly influenced by the historico-literary studies of José Antonio Maravall and the dramatico-structural essays of Alexander A. Parker, especially by the latter's concept of poetic justice. However, if we approach the debate on theatrical licitness of that period with the ideas, perspectives, and prejudgments of these two great scholars of our own, it is possible, even probable, that we may arrive at some conclusions not justified by the actual historical and ideological context. Spanish and Hispanic dramatists were not necessarily reactionaries or conformists, and they did not blindly follow a morality imposed on society by an imperial Church. Instead of sustaining a conformist or moralist image of Calderón or of Salazar y Torres or of Vera Tassis or of Sor Juana, this study of the conflictive context of the debate proves that they fought against the imposition of an ecclesiastical culture that Antonio García Berrio compared to the "uniformidad reglada de convento" (regulated uniformity of a convent [1978, 64]). The cape-and-sword play confirmed that the appropriate morality for priests and professed religious was not necessarily suited to secular or lay persons. Such prejudgments of Golden Age dramatists fail to address their courage in combating the pressures placed on them by the Spanish Comedia's detractors. And it is worthwhile to repeat that the cape-and-sword play, in particular, expressed in many works a vital doctrine appropriate for the laity that duly respected the personal, social, and sacramental importance of human love and matrimony. In this regard, it is also pertinent to recall Foucault's observation in "What Is Enlightenment?": "In the seventeenth century, there was a humanism that presented itself as a critique of Christianity or of religion in general; there was a Christian humanism opposed to an ascetic and much more theocentric humanism" (1984, 44). We have traced the confrontation of a Christian humanism with its more ascetic and theocentric variety.

honor, and the lower classes that neither understand nor sympathize with the motives and behavior of their masters who are tied to those codes. In accordance with the code of honor, the nobleman who does a favor or performs an act that benefits another demonstrates and proves his nobility, especially when he assumes personal risk in carrying it out. The one who benefits from such an act is obligated to his or her benefactor and should express gratitude, first verbally, and then with suitable acts. This system of benefit or kindness and gratitude serves to lay the foundation of society and to assure its proper functioning. In fact, the code of honor is based on the myth of social unity, in which all members of society are linked in their personal interactions through mutual obligations precisely defined according to the place one occupies in the social hierarchy.

There are various interpretations of, or manners of understanding, the requirements of the code of honor that I have described elsewhere as 1) degenerate honor, 2) immature honor, and 3) mature honor (O'Connor 1991). In general, honor obligates the nobleman to serve his neighbor and, in particular, to defend women. In regard to the latter obligation, the antithesis of honor (a clear example of its degeneration or debasement) leads to the rape or death of women, actions that occur, for example, in Calderón's *El alcalde de Zalamea* (The Mayor of Zalamea), *Fortunas de Andrómeda y Perseo* (The fortunes of Andromeda and Perseus), and *El médico de su honra*. In *El encanto,* Don Juan tends to exhibit an immature understanding of the code of honor (one that is primarily egocentric), but in its practice he does not fail to put himself at risk, hastening to Don Diego's side when the latter is attacked in front of Celestina's house. Don Diego, a magnanimous character, demonstrates a more mature, other-centered understanding of the code, especially when he recognizes that Don Juan's saving his life leaves him obligated to his enemy. But the essential conflict that the cape-and-sword play pushes to an extreme concerns what Vera Tassis designated as the "ley paternal" (paternal law [2617]) and the free will of young men and women, concrete and generational representations of the conflictive potential of the codes of honor and love. The tension between generations arises, moreover, from the desire of the young to follow the precepts of the code of love at the same time as their fathers and elders impose the impersonal mandates of the code of honor that have to do with primogeniture, estates, and familial relations and connections.[20] In *El encanto* the rational and emotional confusion experienced

[20] In 1763, an adversary of the dramatic authors of the seventeenth century, José

by the characters on trying to attend simultaneously to various noble obligations results in delightful comedy, particularly in the dueling scene.

THEMATICS, STRUCTURE, AND VARIANT ENDINGS OF *EL ENCANTO ES LA HERMOSURA Y EL HECHIZO SIN HECHIZO / LA SEGUNDA CELESTINA*

Although the principal theme of superstition, especially as a significant dimension in the plot of a cape-and-sword play, may appear to us a bit strange, it is very much at home in the dramatic tradition established by Calderón. Moreover, the handling of the theme by Calderón and Salazar y Torres anticipates a typically eighteenth-century manifestation, the *comedia de magia* based on the character of the male or female magician,[21] which alerts us to its theatrical and social importance in the period.[22] The theme of superstition assists in bonding the other themes to the structure of *El encanto,* because excessive and disordered passion inclines the characters to accept and to believe in whatever promises to fulfill their desires.

Further, the theme of arranged marriages, especially those rejected by the young ladies of the play, becomes linked with our principal

---

Clavijo y Fajardo, criticized the convention of arranged or forced marriages:

> Los padres y los hermanos suelen usar de un despotismo demasiado duro y violento en señalar novios á sus hijas y hermanas, y con tal que á ellos les gusten y hallen sus razones de conveniencia, se obstinan en que lo han de encontrar también á su gusto. Ve aquí una razón para que las pobres muchachas procuren proveerse por otros medios. (Cotarelo 1904, 156a)
>
> [The fathers and brothers are accustomed to applying an excessively harsh and violent despotism in designating fiances for their daughters and sisters, and provided that they like these fellows and find these arrangements convenient, they persist in that they too should find them also to their liking. Here you see the reason why the poor girls seek to provide for themselves by other means.]

This appears to describe the situations of Doña Ana and Doña Beatriz in *El encanto*, especially that of Doña Beatriz, whose father has just departed from Seville bound for Cadiz to marry her there to one of the family's kinsmen. As I have shown in a recent study (O'Connor 1993), the Comedia challenges this convention by establishing conformity or agreement (*la conformidad*) between the bride and groom as the basis for a true marriage, and the spouses who enter into marriage without this conformity run the risk of tragic failure.

[21] See the article of Donald C. Buck and the fundamental book by Julio Caro Baroja.

[22] It is worth recalling that in American history 1692 is the date of the infamous Salem Witch Trials in Massachusetts.

theme of credulous superstition and with the important theme of abuse of paternal authority. The young ladies seek out Celestina the magician as a last recourse in their effort to avoid an emotional and matrimonial pledge not to their liking. Similarly, the motives behind an exaggerated code of honor induce Don Luis to seek out the same deceiver due to his desire to identify the gallant who is threatening the honor (*honra*) of his daughter and family. An arranged or forced marriage serves to illustrate the conflict between generations and, at the same time, underscores a criticism of the exaggerated sense of honor that usually initiates the conflict. The father does not share the personal interests felt by the young, since his have more to do with public opinion, money, nobility, and the reputation of his future son-in-law, in other words, with external interests that ignore the intimate nature of marriage. Calderón severely criticized this abuse of paternal authority and even placed in the mouths of some women, Spanish maidens and classical and mythic infantas, an open complaint against the practice.[23] Consequently, the Spanish court was accustomed to hearing in royal theaters the denunciation of such abuses of power on the part of the older generation, and *El encanto* fits well within this Calderonian tradition, especially pronounced from the time of the marriage of the infanta María Teresa to Luis XIV in 1660 and thereafter.

As the first title of the play suggests, Salazar y Torres envisioned his work as ridiculing superstition, especially the irrational belief in witches. In Calderonian theater there is a long tradition of poking fun at superstition, evidenced in such works as *El astrólogo fingido* (The fake astrologer), *La dama duende* (The Phantom Lady), *El galán fantasma* (The phantom suitor), and *El encanto sin encanto* (Enchantment without enchantment). But it was true inspiration when Salazar incorporated a Celestinesque and magical character into the structure of a cape-and-sword play and, at the same time, maintained a comedic tone throughout the dramatic action.[24] In *El encanto es la hermosura,* Celestina's diabolical fame depends on public opinion that she seeks assiduously to

---

[23] See my study, "*Infantas*, *Conformidad*, and Marriages of State."

[24] Lope de Vega created a masterpiece, *El caballero de Olmedo,* when he incorporated another Celestinesque and "diabolical" character into an apparent cape-and-sword play, that only in Act III definitely becomes tragic. There are, however, indications of the tragic tone throughout the Lopean play, just as there are clear indications of the comedic tone throughout *El encanto,* in the dialogue as well as in stage directions. (For more on stage directions, see A. Hermenegildo's article.) I deal with the "diabolic" nature of Fabia in "The Knight of Olmedo and Oedipus." For prior studies of *El encanto,* see O'Connor 1974 and 1978.

increase. It is ironic that one of the noble's foremost obligations is also to increase his personal and familial honor or reputation. In both cases, however, the arbiter of fame or reputation is the general public, often referred to, with deliberate critical intention, as the ignorant *vulgo* (populace). As is confirmed in Calderonian plays dealing with superstition, the dramatist establishes a structural process that consists of two parts that I have called in *El encanto* the "mythicizing" and "demythicizing" of Celestina (O'Connor 1977). In the mythicizing of Celestina, the other characters witness the power of the deceitful bawd and find no rational explanation for her astrological science, for her magic, or for her witchcraft, or, believing right from the start in her supernatural powers, they become more convinced of them. This part of the process develops until almost the middle of Act III, at which point her demythicizing begins: the moment in which the other characters at last begin to discover Celestina's tricks and deceits, resulting in general disillusionment for all.[25]

In the conclusions of Sor Juana and Vera Tassis this demythicizing is handled well. Vera Tassis's consists of four parts that highlight the fundamentally antimagic and antisuperstitious dimension of his conclusion:

1) The explanation of how Celestina became aware of Don Juan's story and of his love for Doña Ana;
2) The explanation of how Don Juan showed up in Don Luis's house and how he discovered Doña Beatriz there;
3) The explanation of the deceitful use of the mirror in which Doña Ana and Doña Beatriz saw respectively Don Juan and Don Diego;
4) The explanation of how Don Luis twice saw Don Diego and once Don Juan in the same magical mirror.

In the conclusion now credited to Sor Juana, the demythicizing follows the same plot structure, except where the story line has been modified.[26] In the first place, number three is missing, since these magical

[25] On characterizing knowledge (*episteme*) of the sixteenth century, Michel Foucault observes that people felt obliged to accept magic and erudition on the same plane. Calderón's and Salazar y Torres's insistence on causing false magic, and the superstition that flows from it, to lose prestige, evinces a consciousness typical of the seventeenth century. Instead of interpreting "signs and similitudes [that] were wrapped around one another in an endless spiral" (Foucault, *The Order of Things*, 1973, 32), these dramatists set for themselves the task of investigating reality, deciphering its mysteries and deceits, and establishing scientific knowledge as the only basis of secular human life.

[26] According to Mesonero Romanos, the anonymous conclusion is subsequent to

scenes were excised from that finale.[27] Only numbers one and four coincide, and in the latter case only partially; and number two has been divided into two: a) how Don Juan arrived at Don Luis's house; and b) how Don Juan found there the unknown hunter, Doña Beatriz. Sor Juana brings to her demythicizing a fifth element, more precisely handled in this finale than in Vera's, the explanation of how Don Luis appeared before Tacón in Celestina's house in Salazar's portion of Act III (VT 3405–10 and SJ 3433–40).

While the process of demythicizing Celestina is developed expertly by both authors, the same may not be said regarding her mythicizing. Nineteenth-century editors considered Vera Tassis's conclusion to be superior due to the consistent attention and escalating importance given to Celestina's characterization and participation in the action, that is to say, to the suspenseful development of a process initiated by Salazar y Torres and brought to culmination in the magical manipulation of the mirror.[28] Confronting Salazar's unfinished manuscript, Vera Tassis resolved to develop and amplify the dramatic possibilities that the mirror incident suggested to him, and in which Celestina would play the principal role. Whether the four additional uses of the mirror to deceive the gullible constitute an abuse or excess will depend, in the last analysis, on their theatrical effectiveness in producing laughter. On the other hand, Sor Juana decided to eliminate Vera Tassis's mirror incidents altogether and to concentrate on dueling scenes, in which Celestina plays no part. Without doubt, this impoverishment of Celestina's personality diminishes her dramatic stature.[29]

Vera Tassis's, and its author "imitó y descargó de incidentes la conclusión de Vera Tassis" (imitated and cut down on the incidents in Vera Tassis's conclusion [1951, 241 n. 1]).

[27] Although Salazar utilized the "magical" mirror in the part written by him, its elimination from this second conclusion further accentuates the preference given by its author to the pure cape-and-sword formula, without any mixture with the play of magic.

[28] Mesonero Romanos (see n. 26) states that "hemos dado la preferencia á la [conclusión] de este [Vera] por ser más auténtica y acorde con el resto de la comedia" (we have preferred Vera's [conclusion] because it is more authentic and in accord with the rest of the play [1951, 241 n. 1]).

[29] Although critics may fruitfully debate which conclusion is dramatically superior, such discussions have fundamentally to do with generic issues. Guillermo Schmidhuber and Octavio Paz tend to read *La segunda Celestina* as a cape-and-sword play that serves as a harbinger of the dramatic and theatrical successes of *Los empeños de una casa* (see the "Presentation" and Prologue of the 1990 edition). Mesonero Romanos (see n. 28) prefers Vera's conclusion and provides no detailed explanation. Recently, Ermanno Caldera opines that the "*Segunda Celestina* tiene un final soso y estereotipado en tanto que la parte añadida por Vera representa una interesante profundización del tema mágico" (*Segunda Celestina* has a dull and stereotypical

It was inevitable that some difficulty should arise in the dramatic structure as responsibility for the plot passed from one to another author. Vera Tassis experiences from the outset a moment of doubt and insecurity as seen in Doña Beatriz's repetition of part of the story that she previously narrated in Act II. Fortunately such lapses are rare, for he immediately sets about the task of furthering Celestina's characterization as a false witch and unlearned magician. Some minor defects of plot or flaws in dramatic logic appear in vv. 2655–60 (Doña Ana and Doña Beatriz were unaware of Celestina's duping of Don Luis with the mirror in Act II) and in vv. 2693–98 (Celestina's reason for not having warned Don Diego is a bit odd, because Don Luis knew Antonia better even than Celestina herself).

On the whole, Vera Tassis handles the remainder of the plot with assurance and dramatic skill. For example, at the apex of mythicizing Celestina, he introduces into the minds of both Doña Ana and Doña Beatriz certain doubts. Doña Beatriz, the stronger of the two, begins at this point to waver and questions the magical abilities of the supposed witch (vv. 2923–25 and 2952–60); her strong conviction moves Doña Ana also to doubt the veracity of Celestina's tricks (vv. 3375–90). This scrutiny of Celestina's deceits supplies a transition between the two parts of the plot structure. There are other aspects of Vera Tassis's plot, such as the wound that Don Juan receives from Don Diego, that contribute to making the ending uniform and verisimilar. The wound that Don Juan inflicted on Don Diego in front of Doña Ana's house is compensated for by the cut on the hand that the former receives in their duel. In fact, this duel prepares the road to eventual friendship. And the ludicrous mockery of dueling, from verse 3309 on, is handled

---

ending while the part added by Vera represents an interesting exploration of the theme of magic [1989, 315]). This critic approaches the generic question from the point of view of the comedias de magia (plays dealing with magic), insisting on the fact that *El encanto* is an important precursor of the subgenre comedia de magia that will have a great impact, especially in the eighteenth century. Caldera summarizes his position as follows: "Se trata pues, sobre todo gracias a la conclusión de Vera Tassis, de una comedia de magia completa de todos sus ingredientes . . ." (We are dealing, then, thanks above all to Vera Tassis's ending, with a play of magic complete with all its ingredients [321]). My personal position is that Salazar y Torres intended to harmonize two distinct dramatic genres, the cape-and-sword play and the play of magic, by imitating preceding Calderonian models. It is not possible to evaluate the question of superiority without a clear vision of the dramatic logic that informs the play. To speculate on whether Vera Tassis knew in advance how his friend Salazar y Torres intended to conclude the play, while an interesting and exciting question, would prove to be an idle exercise that would, in fact, distract us from the main issue of the play's internal logic and dramatic structure.

with humor and wit.[30] But the final liberating touch added by Vera Tassis arises from Doña Ana's and Doña Beatriz's choosing as husbands the men they like and want, Don Juan and Don Diego. The subtle irony of this situation, with its deliberate rejection of patriarchy's claim to dispose of the lives of one's children, especially of one's daughters, suggests the appropriate role for an at-long-last prudent father: approver, and not the maker, of matches. Since Don Luis had already suspected this was precisely what was going to occur (3364–66), the dramatic irony of the final pairing off also extends to the unsuspecting couples themselves, sparing no one in its intergenerational reach.

On the contrary, the ending attributed to Sor Juana manifests a totally different and, perhaps, erroneous idea of the logical structure of the play. Celestina is a very weak character in this conclusion because she lacks magical grandeur and deceitful panache. Her role appears to have been deliberately minimized in the first part of the ending. In Vera Tassis's version Celestina is the center of all the action, rising to enormous stature and becoming an all-encompassing dramatic force in the mirror incidents with Doña Ana, Doña Beatriz, and Don Luis; in Sor Juana's ending the mythicizing of the bawd is abandoned in order to advance other aspects of Salazar's plot. Sor Juana creates a dramatic action that relies too much on traditional incidents of the cape-and-sword play, in which the young female characters have the most interesting and active parts.[31] Thus, when Doña Ana and Doña Beatriz leave home thickly veiled to frustrate the impending duel, this recourse to a proven convention of the comic genre, the *tapada,* signals not only the future prominence of romantic interests in the play, but also the secondary importance assigned to Celestina and to the theme of magic.

As is to be expected, there are other plot inconsistencies in Sor Juana's ending. When Salazar y Torres ceased writing, Celestina was about to visit Doña Ana and Doña Beatriz. This imminent visit does

---

[30] The mockery of noble codes of conduct, particularly in their automaton-like application to "real-life" situations by some characters, forms part of the cape-and-sword play. In Calderón's *La dama duende,* for instance, the duel in Act III between Don Manuel and Don Luis takes place only by fits and starts, and such Calderonian scenes influenced both Vera Tassis's and Sor Juana's dramatization of the duel between Don Juan, Don Diego, and Don Luis. On the other hand, the cape-and-sword play also presents an idealization of the conduct of noble persons, which constantly confuses their low-class servants. See my study, "La gramática y retórica del honor calderoniano."

[31] One must keep in mind that Golden Age dramatists often wrote for specific theatrical companies, and the latters' strengths and limitations affected in concrete ways the outcome of what to us appears unfettered creativity.

not occur at the beginning of Sor Juana's conclusion, and vv. 2884–91 announce the new direction the play is to take. The principal limitation of this ending arises from the prolongation of action involving the duel, in which Celestina has no part, at the expense of her spellbinding incantations before the mirror, or other magical tricks. From verse 2509 until 3164, Celestina appears only from v. 2871 to 2960, 14% of the total. She is a diminishing presence on stage in proportion to the progressive weakening of her deceitful personality. But more significantly, she fails dramatically by not reaching that high point anticipated by the trajectory of her characterization: Celestina the false magician needs to arrive at the zenith of illusion and deceit, including self-deceit, which does not occur in this ending. In addition, Don Diego lacks Hispanic *hombría* (manliness / courage), due to his desire to overlook, without appropriate satisfaction, the past offense suffered at Don Juan's hands (vv. 2809–18). In contrast with the compensation that Vera Tassis provides for the incident, the fact that in Sor Juana's version Don Juan declares the duel over is very unsatisfying (v. 3499). And, finally, the two noblemen take the initiative in declaring themselves to be the future husbands of their ladies, stifling thereby, Doña Ana's and Doña Beatriz's demand for the basic human right to choose one's spouse. If the cape-and-sword play advances what today is called feminist interests, Sor Juana's hesitating and rejectionist finale reinforces the *parthenoi's* "in between male-identified statuses."

For these reasons, Vera Tassis's version of the play, in spite of its defects, is superior to Sor Juana's. It agrees better with the structure planned and partially executed by Salazar, and its appreciable dramatic, scenic,[32] and comic merits, and better-conceived action, make it a delightful conclusion to *El encanto es la hermosura y el hechizo sin hechizo,* one of the best cape-and-sword plays and plays of magic written in the seventeenth century. On the other hand, the ending attributed to Sor Juana also displays significant dramatic and scenic merits, a fact verified by subsequent editions and by the preference given to it by some modern critics.[33]

[32] P. Manuel Guerra included in his classification of Calderonian works the comedia de santos (saint play). In the production of this kind of Comedia there was a marked use of spectacle that incorporated all the scenographic means then available in Spain's public and private theaters. Although the spectacular dimension of *El encanto* does not equal the usual scenic effects of the great fiestas regias (royal festivities) and comedias de teatro (machine plays), this play signals, nonetheless, the passage of an emphasis on scenic theatricality from a typical genre of the seventeenth century, the comedia de santos, to another that will become quite important in the eighteenth, the comedia de magia.

[33] I wish to express my gratitude and appreciation to Professor Georgina Sabat

THE TWO SALAZARIAN STYLES: *PROLOGUE* AND *PLAY*

In *Orígenes de la novela* (Origins of the novel), Marcelino Menéndez Pelayo observed the following regarding *El encanto es la hermosura:*

> El enredo hábil y entretenido de esta comedia honra a su autor, no menos que la sal y agudeza de los diálogos y la limpieza general del estilo, salvo algún resabio culterano, de que nadie podía librarse entonces. Pero lo más curioso es el tipo de la nueva Celestina, que conserva muchos rasgos de la antigua, y es una especie de adaptación morigerada, para los cosquillosos oídos del tiempo de Carlos II. (1946, 3:241)
>
> [The skillful and entertaining plot of this play honors its author, no less than the wit and sharpness of the dialogues and the general clarity of its style, except some bad habits attributable to the precious style, of which no one was able to free himself at that time. But its most curious aspect concerns this new type of Celestina, who conserves many traits of the old one, and is a kind of restrained adaptation for the touchy ears of the time of Carlos II.]

While the Celestina of *El encanto* exhibits all the decorum expected from dramatists of the second half of the seventeenth century, the criticism of the play's "bad habits attributable to the precious style" requires further explanation. In effect, the Baroque style of Salazar y Torres's mythic plays and of the prologue to *El encanto* yields to a general sim-

---

de Rivers who sent me a photocopy of her article, "Los problemas de *La segunda Celestina*," before its publication in *NRFH*, and photocopies of the newspaper articles of Alejandro Toledo, Antonio Alatorre, Octavio Paz, Guillermo Schmidhuber, José Pascual Buxó, and Luis Leal that appeared in *Proceso* 710, 713, 714, 725, 731, 739, 740, 744, 745, 746 (1990–91); *Vuelta* 169 and 174 (1990–91); *La Jornada Semanal* 76 (1990); and *Nuevo Texto Crítico* 4.7 (1991). Professor Sabat de Rivers encouraged me to examine those aspects of the polemic that were of particular interest to specialists in seventeenth-century Hispanic theater. My first efforts in this regard were kindly received by Margit Frenk, who accepted them for publication in *Literatura Mexicana*. I would like to take this opportunity to express my sincere appreciation to Professor Frenk for her encouragement, interest, and appreciable skills as editor of my article.

The continuing interest in the polemic and in the many issues it has raised also led me to revise substantially an edition of the play with the two variant endings that was originally accepted for publication in 1973 in the series "Clásicos Castellanos," but has yet to appear there.

I would also like to take this opportunity to thank personally and sincerely Professor Guillermo Schmidhuber for having kindly sent me a copy of his edition of *La segunda Celestina* and for a critical and friendly correspondence over the past several years on a topic that is of great and continuing interest to us both.

plicity and clarity in the cape-and-sword play and play of magic. With his typical sense of irony, Salazar y Torres himself calls attention to and, with authorial effacement, gently burlesques the opposition of dramatic styles and tones that stand out so clearly in the contrast of prologue to play, and also within the action of the play itself. Flirting with Doña Beatriz as the action begins, Don Juan adopts an elegant and forced style that highlights the mechanization of his conduct. Doña Beatriz rejects him with a quick retort:

> Retórico forastero,
> excusad cortesanías
> que ni yo escucho ni entiendo. (49–51)
>
> [Rhetorical stranger, / spare me your gallantries / that I neither listen to nor understand.]

It is precisely the rhetorical character of Calderonian drama that some critics in the eighteenth and nineteenth centuries attacked so fiercely. Immediately after this allusion to the falsity and conventionality of the gallant or courteous style, Salazar y Torres has Don Juan deliver a beautiful lament, even much more stylized than before, on the mysterious woman who has just rebuffed him (127–352). And, later in the play, when Don Juan attempts to justify to Doña Ana his flirting with Doña Beatriz in the forest, once again it is emphasized that the acceptance and practice of an exaggerated rhetorical style, a mechanization of human speech, have their counterpart and justification in the equally mechanical deportment of a gallant in the presence of a beautiful lady, any lady: "Esa fue cortesanía" (That was courtesy [1677]).[34]

Perhaps the criticism that Menéndez Pelayo makes of the "resabio culterano" fails to appreciate the truly ironic tone that Salazar adopts with respect to the dramatic styles that are evident throughout the work. Salazar ultimately reminds his audience that every play, but especially the cape-and-sword play, is unreal and depends upon a highly-stylized artistic form, and that the styles employed in displaying that art are equally conventional. The brusque contrast between the styles used in the prologue and play could prove to be particularly shocking for

[34] Having to explain how it is possible to woo and love two ladies at the same time brings out the comic and tragic valences of many plot contrivances in the seventeenth century. In examining Don Gutierre's speech on the difference between the moon and sun (Doña Leonor and Doña Mencía) in *El médico de su honra* (I:520–44), with respect to the theme of verbal mechanization, one finds the tragic counterpart to the comic variety exemplified here.

anyone who does not take into account the conventions that determine and govern their use.

The prologue to *El encanto es la hermosura* imitates the procedures of a poetic competition (*certamen poético*) dramatized by some allegorical figures: on the one hand, Germany, the Heavens, and the Chorus of Lights; and, on the other, Spain, the Earth, and the Chorus of Flowers. The Gongoristic verse is loaded with Baroque stylistic devices and with a typically-Calderonian poetic virtuosity, especially characteristic of court theater. For example, in vv. 1–32 the *correlación paratáctica* (paratactical correlation) of Spain and Germany is transformed, in the responses of the Heavens and Earth, into a *correlación hipotáctica* (hypotactical correlation).[35] In vv. 113–36 one finds an example of the technique *diseminación-recolección* (dissemination-collection or enumeration-recapitulation). In spite of the ostentation and musicality that characterize the prologue to a royal festivity, two groups dispute which of them should celebrate the birthday of Mariana de Austria, a celebration that does not disguise a crude political reality of that time. On 6 November 1675 Mariana's son, Carlos II, became king of Spain, and his incapacity to rule set off a competition between his mother and his bastard half-brother, Don Juan José de Austria. In 1677 the latter deposed Mariana and governed in the name of his brother the king. In 1675, the year in which Salazar penned the prologue, the subject was still a burning question, and only the death of Don Juan José de Austria in 1679 would put a temporary end to these dynastic disturbances. Salazar resolved the conflict poetically, by transforming into cooperation and harmony what was in fact a competition over who was to rule. The conflict between the political rivals of that time, the German and Spanish factions, anticipates and prepares the audience for the conflicts of the play: between generations, between the sexes, among men for the love of a lady, and among women for the love of a man. Although conformity (*conformidad*) between the young gentlemen and ladies would produce a just resolution of the emotional conflicts of the play, only the death of Don Juan José would resolve the political discord broached in the prologue.

[35] See D. Alonso and C. Bousoño's book, in which one finds definitions of and studies dealing with these techniques.

EDITIONS AND PREMIERES OF *EL ENCANTO ES LA HERMOSURA* AND OF *LA SEGUNDA CELESTINA*[36]

The *editio princeps* of Agustín de Salazar y Torres's cape-and-sword play and play of magic, *El encanto es la hermosura y el hechizo sin hechizo,* was published in *Cítara de Apolo* (Apollo's zither) with the conclusion of Vera Tassis, who had edited the two-volume complete works of Salazar. At the end of the seventeenth century a *suelta* edition (single issue)[37] of the other version, titled *La segunda Celestina,* was published in Madrid, but without any notation that the author had not finished the play.[38]

Although *El encanto es la hermosura* was destined to celebrate in Madrid the birthday of Doña Mariana de Austria on 22 December 1675, it is probable that the premiere, with the Vera Tassis ending, was postponed until the following year. In his "Discourse on the Life and Works of Don Agustín de Salazar," Vera explained that the dramatist was writing the royal piece when he died on 29 November 1675. The Mexican premiere of this first version, with the ending by Vera Tassis, probably took place in 1679, the date assigned to the play by Maria y Campos in his *Guía de representaciones teatrales en la Nueva España (siglos XVI al XVIII)* (Guide to theatrical productions in New Spain [Sixteenth to the Eighteenth Centuries]).[39]

The first mention of *La segunda Celestina* occurred in 1682 in an anonymous *Carta en que, con ocasión de haber aprobado el Padre Guerra, de*

---

[36] See my article, "Los enredos de una pieza," for more details on the issues discussed in this section. For a bibliographic study of *Cítara de Apolo*, see O'Connor 1973a. For a study of prior collaboration between Salazar and Vera, see O'Connor 1973b.

[37] This, to the moment, *editio princeps* of the second version of the play is presently located in the rare-book collection of the University of Pennsylvania. Prior to its acquisition by Pennsylvania, it formed part of the collection of Spanish plays of the counts of Harrach, Austrian ambassadors in Madrid at the end of the seventeenth century.

[38] See the bibliography of both versions. See also the complete bibliography that I previously published (O'Connor 1975).

[39] The exact quotation is: "1677, 78 y 79.—Se representan en el Coliseo las comedias de Agustín Salazar y Torres, sobrino del virrey Torres y Rueda, tituladas 'Elegir al enemigo', 'Los juegos olímpicos' 'El encanto es la hermosura' y 'Hechizo sin hechizo', una especie de segunda parte de 'La Celestina', de Fernando de Rojas" (1677, 78, and 79.—There were performed in the Coliseum the plays of Agustín Salazar y Torres, the nephew of the viceroy Torres y Rueda, titled "Elegir al enemigo" [Choosing the enemy], "Los juegos olímpicos" [The Olympic games], and "El encanto es la hermosura" and "Hechizo sin hechizo," a kind of second part of "La Celestina," of Fernando de Rojas [1959, 98]).

la Santísima Trinidad, las comedias del tiempo presente en la 5 Parte de Calderón, dice los inconvenientes que hay en su representación (Letter in which, on the occasion of the approbation of Father Guerra, of the Most Holy Trinity, of the present day's plays in Calderón's Fifth Part, is stated the inconveniences that arise from their performance). The passage reads as follows: "De esto se compone la Comedia: de una tercera—dígalo *La segunda Celestina*—; de un padre celoso—díganlo de Calderón muchas, que en casi todas hay barbas" (Of this the *Comedia* is fashioned: concerning a go-between—let *La segunda Celestina* bear witness—; concerning a jealous father—let many Calderonian plays bear witness, for in almost all of them there are older gentlemen [Vitse 1988, 151]). Does the anonymous author of the letter refer here to the second version of the play or to a popular title by which the first was known? Regrettably, this piece of information tells us only about the popularity of the play and the impact it had on one of its spectators. Nevertheless, in October of 1683 Sor Juana referred three times in the Sainete II of *Los empeños de una casa* to a play entitled *La Celestina,* written in collaboration and performed prior to the production of the former work. It is probable that *La Celestina* was performed between 1679 and 1683 in Mexico, and, due to the same title of a Calderonian play no longer extant,[40] on printing this second version it was assigned at the end of the century the title *La "segunda" Celestina,* the same title given to Salazar's work in 1682 by the anonymous author of the *Carta*. According to available documentation, *La segunda Celestina's* premiere in Madrid took place on Tuesday of Shrovetide (6 March) in 1696, in the Salón de los Reinos of the Buen Retiro Palace (Varey and Shergold 1989, 216). Curiously, and significantly, the piece was referred to by the plain title of *La Celestina* in the documentation published by Shergold and Varey in 1982 (217). It is not known with certainty whether the 1696 date represents that of the premiere in Madrid or simply the repetition of some former production not registered in existing documents.

[40] In various volumes, Vera Tassis mentioned Calderón's *La Celestina,* for example in 1682 (The true fifth part) and in 1691 and 1698 (The ninth part).

ABBREVIATIONS[41]

Aut. = *Diccionario de Autoridades*
En. E-C. = *Enciclopedia Espasa-Calpe*
P. = Padre (Father)
págs. = páginas (pages)
s.ed. = sin editorial (no publisher)
s.f. = sin fecha (no date)
s.l. = sin lugar (no place)

Bibliography of *El encanto es la hermosura y el hechizo sin hechizo*

1681 = In *Cítara de Apolo,* 1681. Loa págs. 239–42; comedia págs. 243–90.
1694 = In *Cítara de Apolo,* 1694. Loa págs. 229–32; comedia págs. 233–79.
H = Suelta. Sevilla: Joseph de Hermosilla, s.f. 36 págs.
BAE = In *Dramáticos posteriores a Lope de Vega.* Ed. Ramón de Mesonero Romanos. Volume 49 of *Biblioteca de Autores Españoles.* Madrid: Atlas, 1951. II: 241–64.
TS = In *Teatro selecto antiguo y moderno nacional y extranjero.* Madrid, 18—. III: 753–87.

Bibliography of *La segunda Celestina*

CH = In *Comedias varias de los Condes de Harrach.* Volume 14 of *Spanish Drama of the Golden Age.* S.l.: s.ed., s.f. Loa [págs. 1–4]; comedia [págs. 5–48].
BNM1 = Suelta. S.l.: s.ed., s.f. [36 págs.][42]
BNM2 = Suelta. S.l.: s.ed., s.f. [41 págs.]

---

[41] A complete bibliography is available in O'Connor 1975. See Sabat de Rivers (1992) for interesting details on the 1694 edition of *Cítara de Apolo.*

[42] BNM1 and BNM2 do not print the prologue, suggesting thereby a date of publication for these texts subsequent to that of CH.

VERSIFICATION OF THE *PROLOGUE* TO *EL ENCANTO ES LA HERMOSURA* AND TO *LA SEGUNDA CELESTINA*[43]

1–16	Letras cantadas con asonancia a-o en los pares (tres octosílabos seguidos por un dodecasílabo)
17–32	letras cantadas con asonancia a-o en los pares (dos octosílabos seguidos por dos decasílabos)
33–112	romances en o-e
113–36	letras cantadas con asonancia o-e en los pares (cuatro grupos de cuatro octosílabos seguidos por dos pentasílabos)
137–70	romances en o-e
171–202	letras cantadas con asonancia í en los pares (cuartetos de decasílabos y dodecasílabos)

VERSIFICATION OF *EL ENCANTO ES LA HERMOSURA* AND OF *LA SEGUNDA CELESTINA*

Act I

1–398	Romances en i-a
399–722	redondillas con rima abrazada (abba)
723–1006	romances en a-a
1007–1202	romances en e-o

Act II

1203–1910	romances en e-a
1911–2296	romances en ó

Act III

2297–2324	silvas de consonantes (silvas pareadas)
2325–2508	romances en a-o

The Vera Tassis Conclusion

2509–2972	romances en i-a
2973–3574	romances en e-o

The Conclusion Attributed to Sor Juana

2509–2604	redondillas con rima abrazada (abba)
2605–2960	romances en e-o
2961–3336	romances en i-o
3337–3512	redondillas abrazadas (abba)

[43] To assist the reader, the versification also appears in brackets in the text of the work.

EDITORIAL CRITERIA

This edition is based on the text found in 1681 because it is closest in time to the Salazarian autograph, which was subsequently corrected and polished by Vera Tassis. The base edition of the ending attributed to Sor Juana is CH, and I suspect that, although it may be derived from the autograph, it represents either its uncorrected stage or a copy made from the autograph for performance purposes.[44] The orthography, accentuation, and punctuation of the two texts have been modernized, although some contractions have been retained ("deste" = "de este" [*loa* v. 139], "esotros" = "esos otros" [v. 955]) and some archaic forms ("prompta" = "pronta" [*loa* v. 80], "propria" = "propia" [VT v. 2776], "invidiaba" = "envidiaba" [v. 252]). Typical forms of the period have also been maintained, such as "quien" = "que" (that refers to "pulgas" or fleas [v. 2302]), "quién" = "quiénes" (VT v. 3082), or the various uses of "donde" and "adonde" (vv. 58 y 1717). The variable use of direct and indirect pronouns has also been respected: "la" instead of "le" (v. 9 and VT v. 2802), "le" instead of "lo" (v. 428), etc. When "porque" = "para que," it is written as two words ("por que") and it is duly noted in the margin [*loa* v. 48]. At times the scansion requires that the second syllable of "porque" be stressed, and in these cases also the word is divided into two and a note to this effect appears in the margin.[45] All asides are given in parentheses "(. . .)" with "[*Aparte*]" in square brackets at the beginning. Parenthetical phrases appear within dashes "—. . . . . .—." Anything introduced by the editor into 1681 or CH is indicated by square brackets. In addition to numbering the verses, I supply the versification in the margin and divide the acts into dramatic *cuadros,* "scenes," defined according to Spanish practice at that time.

Although I hope that specialists will not be disappointed with the present eclectic edition, they should take into consideration that the editorial apparatus has as its final aim the clarification of the poetic and dramatic text and the facilitation of its use by North American students who are not experts in Spanish classical theater. In advance I beg the latters' indulgence for my pedagogical zeal, that may seem to them to be excessive or unduly punctilious, but that I judge to be necessary so that the former may also appreciate and enjoy this Salazarian text.

---

[44] See appendix 1, which compares the state of these two texts.

[45] Vera Tassis frequently provides the correct scansion, giving in 1681 "porque" as "porquè" (VT v. 3311).

JORNADA SEGUNDA, ESCENA XXI.

SALAZAR Y TORRES (16).

EL ENCANTO ES LA HERMOSURA.

LA SEGUNDA CELESTINA (a).

LOA

para la comedia

de

EL ENCANTO ES LA HERMOSURA

Y EL HECHIZO SIN HECHIZO

Representóse a los años de la reina

nuestra señora doña Mariana de Austria.

De don Agustín de Salazar y Torres

PERSONAS

ALEMANIA	CIELO
ESPAÑA	TIERRA
CORO DE LUCES	CORO DE FLORES

Sale ALEMANIA cantando lo que se sigue.

ALEMANIA *¡Ah del cielo, donde hermoso* [*letras cantadas*]
el sol en luciente espacio
brilla, quema, vive, luce
con llamas, con fuego, con luces, con rayos!

[*Sale ESPAÑA cantando lo que se sigue.*]

ESPAÑA *¡Ah de la tierra, que hermosa*
en su fecundo teatro
abre, viste, cría, pule

las fuentes, los montes, las fieras, los prados!

ALEMANIA *Oye mi voz que festiva*
para el empeño más alto
llama, pide, quiere, busca
la luna, los signos, la aurora, los astros.

ESPAÑA *Mi voz escucha que alegre*
al empeño más sagrado
une, junta, mezcla, sigue
tus plantas, tus selvas, tus flores, tus prados.[1]

ALEMANIA *¡Ah del cielo!*

Sale el CIELO *cantando.*

CIELO *Ya del cielo*
te escucha el ardor que ufano
brilla con llamas, quema con fuego,
vive con luces, luce con rayos.

ESPAÑA *¡Ah de la tierra!*

Sale la TIERRA *cantando.*

TIERRA *La tierra*
te oye cuyo adorno vario
abre las fuentes, viste los montes,
cría las fieras, pule los prados.

CIELO *¿Por qué, Alemania felice,*
tu süave acento grato
llama la luna, pide los signos,
quiere la aurora, busca los astros?

TIERRA *¿Por qué, España generosa,*
armonioso tu cuidado
une las plantas, junta las selvas,
mezcla las flores, sigue los prados?[2]

---

[1] Reproduzco la estructura métrica dada en CH para estas letras cantadas, que me parece mejor por preservar la asonancia a-o en los versos pares. En 1681 y 1694 los versos 4, 8, 12 y 16 aparecen como hexasílabos.

[2] Sigo la estructura dada en CH para estas letras cantadas, que, como arriba, mantiene la asonancia a-o en los pares. En 1681 vv. 19, 20, 23, 24, 27, 28, 31 y 32 aparecen como dos pentasílabos cada uno, mientras que en 1694 sólo vv. 19 y 20 aparecen como pentasílabos. La variedad de presentación, que no cambia la estructura poética y musical básica, indica que el esquema impreso dependía, a veces, del capricho del cajista particular.

Representa ALEMANIA.

ALEMANIA Pues atiende . . . [*romances*]

Representa ESPAÑA.

ESPAÑA Pues escucha . . .
ALEMANIA . . . luminosa esfera adonde
logra su imperio la inmensa
majestad de resplandores.
ESPAÑA . . . fecunda madre de cuanta
hermosa copia de flores
a tus campañas ofrecen
fragrantes[3] inudaciones.
ALEMANIA Ya sabes—pues ocupaste
tus brillantes atenciones
en este milagro—como
en el feliz horizonte
de Alemania, que soy yo,
tuvo su oriente el más noble,
más puro, más claro sol,
que es Mariana, por que* logren para que
inmortal eterno día,
después de funesta noche,[4]
ilustrados de sus luces
gloriosamente los hombres.
ESPAÑA Ya sabes—pues fuiste tú
quien, para mirar entonces
mi fortuna, abriste a un tiempo
por ojos todas las flores—
que, siendo yo España, soy
la que he logrado en conformes
dichas la rosa más bella,
la flor más pura y más noble
que el suelo alemán produjo,

[3] "Fragante" y "fragrante" se usaban intercambiablemente en la época. La palabra varía en todas las ediciones. En los vv. 119, 166 y 175 se reza "fragantes," etc. por falta de espacio al final de cada línea.

[4] Felipe IV murió en 1665.

por que* en el mío la adornen para que
devotamente rendidos
los afectos españoles.

ALEMANIA Pues hoy el más feliz día,
de luces más superiores,
ofrece en Mariana bella
astro benigno a los orbes.
Hoy, que en su giro luciente
el sol sus luces esconde
y brevemente discurre
con luceros inferiores,
es el día deseado
en que, atento el sol, recoge
sus rayos porque le ilustran
más soberanos candores.[5]

ESPAÑA Pues hoy es el día en que
se repiten mis honores,
y la memoria festiva
prompta* a celebrarlas[6] corre, pronta
confesando que te debe
los triunfos que reconoce,
pues cada natal florido
es número a mis blasones.

ALEMANIA Y para que tú concurras
con dulces aclamaciones
a festejar este día,
mi acento los aires rompe.

ESPAÑA Y a celebrar esta dicha
te solicitan mis voces,
acordemente obsequiosas
y obsequiosamente acordes.

CIELO Con justa razón me llamas,
Alemania, por que* noten para que
que al reino de la luz toca
aplaudir los resplandores.

TIERRA Con razón tu voz me llama,

[5] Los vv. 65–76 aluden al solsticio de invierno (del 21 al 22 de diciembre) y al natalicio de Mariana (el 22 de diciembre).

[6] Se debe entender "las fiestas," y de esta manera se evita una redundancia con "festiva" del verso anterior.

España feliz, adonde
sólo celebre a la rosa
la esfera de los olores.

CIELO Pues ¿cómo te opones tú . . .
TIERRA ¿Cómo tú, dime, te opones . . .
CIELO . . . a que yo pierda una dicha . . .
TIERRA . . . a que una dicha malogre . . .
CIELO . . . que es bien que se nombre mía?
TIERRA . . . que es bien que mía se nombre?
CIELO Porque hay razón.
TIERRA Porque hay causa.
LAS DOS ¿Pues cuál es?
CIELO Escucha.[7]
TIERRA Oye.
CIELO Y tú, que me has invocado,
favorece a mis razones.
TIERRA Y tú, a cuyo acento vine,
atiende también mis voces.

Canta CIELO.

CIELO *Rayos numeren felices,* *[letras cantadas]*
bellos repitan candores
los años de un sol divino,
porque al sol le corresponden
rayos felices,
bellos candores.

Canta TIERRA.

TIERRA *Mayos expliquen fragrantes,*
suaves le cuenten olores
a la reina flor los años,
pues años de flor componen
mayos fragrantes,
suaves olores.
CIELO *Astros festejen lucientes,*
luces publiquen conformes

---

[7] Dialefa entre "Escucha" y "Oye".

la majestad de la aurora,
porque es luz que anima dócil[8]
astros lucientes,
luces conformes.

TIERRA *Rosas ofrezcan festivas,*
gratas consagren las flores
culto a la real[9] *primavera,*
pues su imperio reconocen
rosas festivas,
gratas las flores.

Representa CIELO.

CIELO Pues ya habrás reconocido [*romances*]
de mis acentos veloces
que el aplauso deste día
a mi razón corresponde.

ALEMANIA Dices bien, porque se hallan
misteriosas proporciones
en que los años del sol
se aplaudan con esplendores.

TIERRA También habrás advertido
de mis cláusulas acordes
que me tocan deste día
festivas veneraciones.

ESPAÑA Bien dices, pues es preciso
con amantes prevenciones
que los años de una flor
sólo a fragrancias se noten;
pero aguarda, que también
son las flores arreboles
de la tierra, pues brillantes
lucen fragrancias las flores.

ALEMANIA Tú también suspende amante
las reverentes cuestiones,
pues son del cielo los astros
bellos floridos ardores.

---

[8] La asonancia o-i no destruye el esquema o-e; es una licencia poética.
[9] Sinéresis en "real".

ESPAÑA Y así, las flores unidas . . .
ALEMANIA Y así, las luces conformes . . .
LAS DOS . . . en bella unión festejamos . . .
ESPAÑA . . . de una luz años y flores . . .
ALEMANIA . . . de una flor años y luces . . .
LAS DOS . . . que fragancia y luz componen.
ALEMANIA Y así, llama tú a las luces.
ESPAÑA Y así, llama tú a las flores.
CIELO Y TIERRA Bien habéis dicho, y por eso
dirán dulces nuestras voces . . .

Canta el CIELO.

CIELO *De ese trono de ardores divinos,* [*letras cantadas*]
estrellas hermosas, llegad y venid,
y, constantes, amantes, brillantes,
con voces de luz a la luz aplaudid.

Canta la TIERRA.

TIERRA *De la esfera fragrante del mayo,*
oh flores hermosas, llegad y salid;
y, olorosas, gustosas, vistosas,
con voces de olor a la flor os rendid.

Sale cantando el CORO DE LUCES.

CORO DE LUCES *Al imperio de luz soberana*
venimos, dejando el ardiente cenit,
y, obedientes, lucientes, ardientes,
ya el claro abrasar se ha mudado en lucir.

Sale cantando el CORO DE FLORES.

CORO DE FLORES *Al precepto de dulces cadencias*
venimos, dejando el alcázar de abril,
y, entre amores, albores y olores,
la rosa te adora, te sirve el jazmín.

Canta ALEMANIA.

ALEMANIA *A los años de flor luminosa*
consagre tu culto oloroso festín,
y, inmortales, reales, leales,
celebren las flores la luz del zafir.

Repítese esta copla por toda la MUSICA, *y dan principio al sarao.*[10]

Canta ESPAÑA.

ESPAÑA *Los candores festejen floridos*
la luz superior, porque siempre feliz
favorece, enriquece, ennoblece
luciente la flor y fragrante el rubí.

Canta TIERRA.

TIERRA *Y vos, Carlos, clavel siempre augusto*
y sol siempre claro,[11] *eterno vivid,*
y cinceles, pinceles, laureles
ocupen del sol el brillante confín.

Canta CIELO.

CIELO *Y vuestra amante unión reverente*
de olor y de luz . . . mas la voz cese aquí,
temerosa, dudosa, obsequiosa,
pues calla discreto quien teme decir.

Repítase la primera copla por toda la MUSICA, *y se dará fin.*

---

[10] *Sarao*—"Junta de personas de estimacion y gerarchía, para festejarse con instrumentos, y bailes cortesanos. Tómase por el mismo báile, ò danza entre muchos" (*Aut*).

[11] Dialefa entre "claro" y "eterno".

EL ENCANTO ES LA HERMOSURA

Y EL HECHIZO SIN HECHIZO

Comedia famosa,

Fiesta al cumplimiento de años

de la Reina nuestra señora doña Mariana de Austria

De don Agustín de Salazar y Torres

PERSONAS

DOÑA ANA	DON JUAN
DOÑA BEATRIZ	DON DIEGO
ANTONIA, CRIADA	DON LUIS, VIEJO
CELESTINA	TACÓN, CRIADO
MUÑOZ, CRIADO	[JUSTICIA]
INÉS, CRIADA	

JORNADA PRIMERA

CUADRO I

Sale DOÑA BEATRIZ en traje de cazadora, con escopeta y sombrero con plumas, retirándose de DON JUAN, que sale siguiéndola, vestido de camino.

DOÑA BEATRIZ Caballero, si adelante [*romances*]
pasáis, haréis que mi[1] ira
con la voz desta escopeta
responda a vuestra osadía.
DON JUAN Bella deidad destos bosques,
émula hermosa de Cintia*, Artemisa o Diana
que para fieras y[2] hombres
el plomo y la voz fulminas;
a quien el Betis* la debe Guadalquivir
cuantas estampas floridas
tus negros ojos encienden,
tu blanco pie resucita;[3]
permítele a un albedrío
que el rendido impulso siga
de adoración voluntaria,
sin dejar de ser precisa.
¿En qué te ofende quien sólo
a seguir tu luz aspira?
¿En qué te agravia?
DOÑA BEATRIZ No más,
que, aunque disculpar podría
vuestro atrevimiento el traje,
pues de vos no conocida
puedo ser, por forastero,

---

[1] Dialefa entre "mi" e "ira".

[2] Dialefa entre "y" y "hombres". También se puede poner diéresis en "fieras".

[3] Las flores al margen del río o brotan debido a la luz de sus ojos negros o vuelven a brotar por el simple contacto con sus pies blancos.

basta que una mujer pida
que no la sigáis, pues es
cierto que no necesita
de otra recomendación
para ser obedecida
que el ser mujer; y si acaso
no cesare la porfía
de seguirme, habrá de ser
del pedernal[4] a las iras
para vuestro atrevimiento
corto castigo la vida;
y así, mirad . . .

DON JUAN Tente, espera,
que obedecerte quería,
pero ya con tu amenaza
disculpo mi grosería;
porque el morir a tus manos
no es desgracia, sino dicha;
pues si al rayo de metal
la nevada mano aplicas,
aun lo irracional conoce
felicidad la rüina:
mira qué harán los humanos
que de tus ojos peligran
a más hermoso instrumento,
con menos ruidosa herida.

DOÑA BEATRIZ Retórico forastero,
excusad cortesanías
que ni yo escucho ni entiendo;
yo me retiro a mi quinta,
donde hay honor que la guarde;
y si sois, como me avisa
vuestro traje, caballero,
quedaos; no de vos se diga
que hay caballero que niega
adonde hay dama que pida.

---

[4] Se refiere al pedernal de la escopeta que, al provocar chispas, dispara la bala ("el plomo" del v. 8). La escopeta sería, entonces, un "rayo de metal" (v. 41) al descargar. *Rayo*—"Metaphoricamente llaman al arma de fuego, por la semejanza al estruendo y estrago que causa el rayo meteóro" (*Aut.*).

Vase, y sale TACON.

DON JUAN Aguarda, detente, espera.
TACON ¿Que haya borracho que sirva
a amo que se pierde y que es
siempre una cosa perdida?
DON JUAN Pues me hallas de buen humor.
TACON Pues dime, pese a mi vida,
¿si he rodeado[5] cuatro leguas
en una mula maldita,
mohina, en fin, aunque hoy tiene
causa para estar mohina,[6]
no quieres que me lamente?
DON JUAN Tacón, de tus boberías
ya te he dicho que me canso.

Sale MUÑOZ.

MUÑOZ ¡Señor! Cierto que gran dicha
ha sido hallarte los dos.
DON JUAN ¡Muñoz!
MUÑOZ En alas venía
de mi cuidado, creyendo
que llegaras a esa villa
solo.
DON JUAN Así, Muñoz, lo creo
de tu buena ley.
TACON La mía
debe de ser de algún turco;
y es verdad, pues cada día,
queriendo ser buen cristiano,
tus cosas me desbautizan*. irritan
DON JUAN ¡Vive Dios, que si no callas
que haré que paguen tus frías
necedades mis pesares!
MUÑOZ ¿Qué cuidado te fatiga

---

[5] Sinéresis en "rodeado".

[6] Juego de palabras o antanaclasis. *Mohina*: 1) mula hija de caballo y burra, y 2) triste, a causa del mal trato recibido de Tacón. También describe la bestia de pelo negro, especialmente en el hocico.

ahora, señor, nuevamente,
cuando alegrarte debía,
después de tan larga ausencia,
el llegar hoy a Sevilla
tu patria? Dinos si[7] es
temer que otra vez te rindan
los halagos de doña Ana,
que un amor tarde se olvida,
si es verdadero.

DON JUAN No[8] es
de ese incendio las reliquias
las que hoy encienden mi pecho;
porque de sus tiranías
estoy tan desengañado
que ni acordarme querría
de su nombre.

TACON Pues yo sé
cuando por nombrarla había
más Anas en tus razones
que en cuatro tapicerías.[9]

DON JUAN ¿No quieres callar?

MUÑOZ Acaso,
¿ha tenido la noticia
de que vienes tu enemigo?[10]

DON JUAN Mucho[11] es que eso me digas,
Muñoz, cuando me conoces,
porque a mí nada me implica
que lo sepa o no lo sepa.

MUÑOZ Pues ¿qué aventura en un día
te ha podido suceder
que te suspenda y aflija
y nosotros no sepamos?

DON JUAN Si en referirlo se alivia
tal vez un cuidado, quiero

---

[7] Dialefa entre "si" y "es".

[8] Dialefa entre "No" y "es".

[9] Dilogía basada en el nombre de doña Ana y "Cierta medída con que se miden las tapicerías" (*Aut.*).

[10] El enemigo a quien se refiere será don Diego.

[11] Dialefa entre "mucho" y "es".

daros del mío noticia:
ya sabéis cómo doña Ana
de Ribera, mi enemiga . . .

MUÑOZ Por que* más cerca murieses, para que
junto a tu casa vivía
en poder de un tío suyo,
mientras su padre venía
en la flota de un gobierno,
con que antes pasó a las Indias.

DON JUAN Amante, pues, de sus luces,
a la continua porfía
de mis quejas, al anhelo
de mis suspiros, propicia
vine a tener su deidad:
¡Oh cuánto el ruego conquista!
No digo bien, la fortuna;
que en bellezas peregrinas,
para conseguir favores,
no hay méritos, sino dichas.
Amante y correspondido
ondas sulcaba* tranquilas surcaba
en los piélagos de amor,
cuando una noche enemiga,
que iba a hablarla por la reja
de un jardín, hallo que hacían
seña a un hombre que embozado
—¡no sé cómo lo repita!—
se llegó a hablarla a la reja,
pero la voz tan remisa
que nada percebir pude;
bien que el alma me decía:
ésa es doña Ana,[12] ése es
amante que solicita
sus favores y tu muerte.
¡Ah villana tiranía
de los celos, pues que matas
sólo con lo que imaginas!
Dígalo yo, pues celoso,

[12] Dialefa entre "Ana" y "ése" o "ése" y "es".

que, con que celoso diga,
está bien exagerada
o la razón o la[13] ira,
embestí con mi contrario,
y a breve rato una herida
recibió; luego al rüido,
advirtiendo que venía
gente y que sacaban luces,
fue en los dos cosa precisa
el retirarnos, por que*[14] para que
no pudiese la malicia
colegir contra doña Ana
alguna sospecha indigna.
Nunca pude averiguar
quién fuese el que se oponía
a mi amor, con que el despecho
me obligó que a pocos días
determinase pasar
a Flandes, sin dar noticia
a la causa de mis daños,
por no encontrar con su vista
satisfacción a mi agravio,
que, en ofensas conocidas,
es infamia el procurarla,
y el procurarla es pedirla.
Tres años estuve en Flandes,
hasta que ha sido precisa
mi vuelta a Sevilla, a causa
de que mis deudos me avisan
que de un mayorazgo, que
de mi parte se litiga,
importaba mi asistencia
para afianzar mi justicia;

---

[13] Dialefa entre "la" e "ira". Véase v. 2.

[14] Conjunción final equivalente a "para que". El acento rítmico cae sobre "que". El uso es común en la época. En *Fineza contra fineza* (1671) de Calderón, el siguiente verso, "venid conmigo, porque" (2106a), también es octosilábico aunque se escribe "porque". Aun cuando no termina un verso, escribo la conjunción como "por que". Para una práctica diferente, véase "Y porque del homenaje / te asegure mi presencia" (2115b) de la misma obra calderoniana.

y en esta última jornada,
para no entrar con el día
en la ciudad, excusando
cumplimientos y visitas,
me adelanté de vosotros
a sestear en la orilla
de Guadalquivir; aquí
empieza la peregrina
historia de otro suceso
de que no tenéis noticia.
Sesteando, pues, del Betis
en la ribera florida,
llegué a un bosque tan süave,
por la sonora armonía
de las aves, tan fragrante,
por los ámbares que espiran
las rosas, que mal pudiera
distinguir veloz la vista
unas flores que cantaban
de unos pájaros que olían.
Absorto y confuso estaba
entre aromas y armonías,
cuando un lento estruendo escucho
entre las ramas vecinas
que, negando el paso al sol,
verde sombra eran del día.
La vista aplico por unas
tenaces hiedras que hacían
maridaje con los sauces,
y lentamente movían
cuantos verdes corazones,
cuando el viento los irrita,
temerosamente laten,
vistosamente palpitan.
Una hermosa cazadora
era la que discurría
lo enmarañado del bosque,
tan bella, tan peregrina . . .
mas querer encarecerla,
más que aplauso, es grosería;
que no es grande la hermosura

que es capaz de encarecida,[15]
ni el pensamiento pudiera
—que es quien más perfecto pinta—
bosquejar de sus reflejos
aun las luces más remisas,
pues contra el común concepto,
sólo en su beldad se mira
una perfección que es menos
imaginada que vista.
Era el exterior adorno
del justillo y la basquiña
azul y plata que, ya
que algún color se permita
a la hermosura del cielo,
pareció cosa precisa
que, habiéndose de vestir,
del mismo cielo se vista.
Azules y blancas plumas
los bellos rizos matizan,
que las insignias de Marte
ya eran de Venus insignias.
Pero de las negras trenzas,
noche que invidiaba el día,
entre el penacho mezcladas
en confusión peregrina,
a la discreción del viento
que mansamente respira,
volaban trenzas y plumas,
que unas peina y otras riza.
Lo licencioso del traje
el pequeño pie a la vista
en dos átomos permite,
y dijo el alma rendida:
"Ya conozco que eres sol,
pues los átomos animas".[16]

---

[15] Elipsis de "ser" ("ser encarecida").

[16] Antanaclasis: *Atomo*—"Se llama por ponderación qualquier cosa pequéña: y en especiál lo usan mucho los Poétas". *Repara en un átomo*—"Se dice del que nota las acciones mas pequéñas, y que no se deben reparar" (*Aut.*). Por consiguiente, se ve muy poco del pie. *Atomos*—"Se suelen llamar por su pequeñéz las motícas que andan

Pero tan imperceptibles,
celosas los encubrían
pequeñas rosas de nácar
que, cuando las solicita
más descubrir el deseo,
si por la selva florida
mueve las ligeras plantas,
apenas se distinguía
la flor del lazo que[17] huella
de la misma flor que pisa.[18]
Una grabada escopeta
la diestra mano fulmina,
dando a entender su hermosura
que, por que* nada se exima para que
de lo humano ni lo bruto,
lleva en armas indecisas
el plomo para las fieras,
para los hombres la vista.
Cansada, pues, de dar muerte
o cansada de dar vida
a las flores y a los brutos,
que unas con la[19] huella anima[20]
y otros con el plomo[21] hiere,
a la margen se reclina
de un arroyo, cuyas ondas,
fulminadas de su vista,
cristalinas llamas vierten,
centellas nevadas rizan.
No hubo flor en la ribera
que no llore su rüina;

---

por el áire tan imperceptibles que solo las vemos al rayo del Sol quando entra por los resquicios de las ventánas, y las llaman átomos del Sol" (*Aut.*).

[17] Dialefa entre "que" y "huella".

[18] Es difícil distinguir el pie, que se parece a una flor, de la flor que pisa al correr. *Lazo*—"Tomase freqüentemente por lo mismo que Lazáda". *Lazada*—"Cierta atadúra que se forma con cinta, cuerda ò cosa semejante, haciendo primero un nudo apretado, del qual nacen quatro como hojas, y queda en forma de flor ò estrella" (*Aut.*).

[19] Dialefa entre "la" y "huella"; véase v. 273.

[20] La huella de ella produce una flor; véanse vv. 10–12.

[21] Dialefa entre "plomo" y "hiere".

mas ¿qué esperaban las flores
cuando las ondas ardían?
De las destrozadas fieras,
las blancas manos teñidas
lava en el cristal undoso,
sin que el cristal las distinga;
corta el agua y, más que aljófar,
blancas centellas salpica,
de cuyo ardor las arenas
fueron doradas cenizas.
Con la mano enciende el agua,
sin valerse de su vista,
que eran ociosos los rayos
donde la nieve encendía.
Yo, pues, en tantos ardores
la llama busqué enemiga,
porque en riesgos tan hermosos
aun son los peligros dichas.
Y así, al dejar el arroyo,
me determiné a seguirla
y hablarla; bien que, al mirarla,
torpes, tardas y remisas
fueron mis voces, por que*[22] porque
un amor mejor se explica
cuando no acierta a explicarse,
que en su dulce tiranía
las palabras mal formadas
son señas de bien sentidas.
Pero ella a mis rendimientos,
hermosa, airada, entendida,
me respondió: "¿Quién ha dicho
que nunca han hecho armonía
esquivez, beldad e ingenio?
Sólo lo contrario digan
las vulgares opiniones;
porque, siendo preferida
la porción del alma al cuerpo,

[22] Aunque es una conjunción causal, el acento rítmico cae sobre la segunda sílaba de "porque," manteniendo el octosílabo.

imperfección fuera indigna
una perla mal labrada
y una concha muy pulida".
Hermosa y discreta, —vuelvo
a decir— que no la siga
me manda, ni a mí me fuera
posible; pues de la quinta
adonde se retiraba
salieron a recibirla
cazadores o criados.
Con que hoy me espera en Sevilla
lo embarazoso de un pleito,
de un enemigo las iras,
de doña Ana las traiciones
y de una beldad esquiva
el nuevo amor imposible;
porque, aunque ya de su vista
me ausenté, si va en el alma
impresa, no es medicina
el que[23] huya del acero
cuando ya llevo la herida.

MUÑOZ De todos esos cuidados,
yo apostaré que la ninfa
que has encontrado en la selva
es el que más te lastima.

TACON Eso está puesto en razón,
que, en buena filosofía,
de las damas y la sarna,
la última es la que más pica.

MUÑOZ Es verdad.

DON JUAN En este caso
quisiera tener noticia
de quién es y que supiera
que su belleza rendida
dejó un alma que no ignore
los trofeos de su vista;
que si ignora la victoria,
¿de qué le sirve el que rinda?

---

[23] Dialefa entre "que" y "huya".

MUÑOZ Pues supuesto que no es más
que eso lo que solicitas,
ya tengo medio con que
lo que deseas consigas.
Hay en Triana[24] una mujer,
que puede ser que ahora viva
donde yo la conocí,
que es hija de Celestina
y heredera de sus obras.
Esta, no hay dama en Sevilla
que no conozca, por que* porque
con las más introducida
está, por su habilidad,
pues vendiendo bujerías*, mercaderías
como abanicos, color,
alfileres, barros, cintas,
guantes y valonas, y otras
semejantes baratijas,
se introduce; y con aquesto
por el ojo de una tía
meterá un papel, y hará
con tan rara y peregrina
maña un embuste que muchos,
siendo así que eso es mentira,
la tienen por hechicera.

TACON ¿Luego no lo es?

MUÑOZ No.

TACON ¿Que digas
eso? Ahora, a mí me deja
que sus virtudes prosiga.

DON JUAN Prosigue, que, por hacer
tiempo, oiré tus boberías.

TACON Celestina, entre las raras [*redondillas*]
mañas con que se introduce,
es la que más se le luce
ser remendona de caras.
Hace caireles*, y en ellos pelucas
entabla una pretensión,

---

[24] *Triana*—"Barrio de Sevilla, famoso por su típico carácter" (*En. E-C.*).

porque entonces la ocasión
la coge por los cabellos.
Pule cejas y pestañas,
y ella introdujo el estilo
de pelar la tez con hilo,
y dél hace sus marañas.
Friega un rostro de manera,
con una y otra invención,
que una cara de Alcorcón[25]
la vuelve de Talavera.[26]
Arrugas quita sin tasa,
y desto yo soy testigo,
a una vieja como un higo
alisó con una pasa.
Hace tan raro jabón
con el sebo y con la[27] hiel,
que hará mano de papel
una mano de tejón.
Es del amor mandadera,
mas su mayor interés
sólo se funda en que[28] es
tan grandísima hechicera,
que a un hombre desde Carmona[29]
le puso en el Preste Juan;[30]
y otro trajo de Tetuán,[31]
como pudiera una mona.
Pero entre una y otra tacha
tiene, hablando la verdad,
una buena habilidad,

---

[25] *Alcorcón*—"En la provincia y diócesis de Madrid. . . . Dista de Madrid 13 kms. y 7 de Getafe . . . y está situada en una eminencia, cerca y á la izquierda de la carretera de Extremadura. . . . Es importante en esta población la industria alfarera" (*En. E-C.*).

[26] *Talavera*—Ciudad de la provincia de Toledo famosa por su cerámica y porcelana. Quiere decir que Celestina hace la cara más fina y lisa.

[27] Dialefa entre "la" e "hiel".

[28] Dialefa entre "que" y "es".

[29] *Carmona*—Ciudad de la provincia de Sevilla.

[30] *Preste Juan*—Preste Juan de las Indias; actualmente parte de la República de China.

[31] *Tetuán*—Ciudad de Marruecos.

que es grandísima borracha.
Pues en esta historia breve
que mi ingenio te describe,
si es asombro como vive,
es un pasmo como bebe.
Y, en fin, aquesta embustera
tiene en amor tal poder
que, si quiere, ha de querer
uno, que quiera o no quiera:
hace amar.

DON JUAN ¡Qué desvarío!

TACON ¿Luego no me crees?

DON JUAN ¡Que sea
tal tu ignorancia que crea
que se fuerza el albedrío!

TACON ¿No crees sus hechicerías?
Pues tú lo verás después.

DON JUAN ¡Qué proprio* del vulgo[32] es propio
creer estas boberías!

MUNOZ Ella es mujer tan estraña,
que esto en toda la ciudad
se cree, siendo habilidad
solamente.

DON JUAN ¡Si su maña
quién es la dama supiera
que ocasiona mi cuidado,
y ya papel o recado
de mi parte introdujera!
Un gran gusto me habéis hecho.

MUÑOZ Si no más que en eso está,
de que ella al punto lo hará
puedes quedar satisfecho;
su casa está en el camino
al entrar en la ciudad.

TACON Allá verás si es verdad
que es bruja.

DON JUAN ¿Ese desatino,
necio, quieres tú que crea?

---

[32] Dialefa entre "vulgo" y "es".

Vamos, pues, sea ella instrumento
para conseguir mi intento,
y lo que se fuere sea.

TACON En fin, ¿que no es bruja?

MUÑOZ No

TACON ¿Ni encantadora?

MUÑOZ Tampoco.

TACON ¿Ni hechicera?

MUNOZ Calla, loco.

TACON Pues así lo fuera yo.[33] *Vanse.*

CUADRO II

Sale CELESTINA.

CELESTINA La que vive de su oficio,
trabaje; que en verdad
es mala la ociosidad,
que, en fin, es madre del vicio.
Al verme cargada de años,
en ser medianera di,
porque en efecto algo en mí
han de obrar los desengaños.
En este oficio una[34] higa
le daré a quien lo inventó;[35]
bien sé yo lo que sé yo
en él, aunque yo lo diga.
La memoria ver intento

---

[33] Recuerdo e imitación del final de la primera jornada de *La dama duende* de Calderón de la Barca.

[34] Dialefa entre "una" e "higa".

[35] *Higa*—"Se llama tambien la accion que se hace con la mano cerrado el puño, mostrando el dedo pulgár por entre el dedo índice y el de enmedio, con la qual se señalaba à las personas infâmes y torpes, ò se hacía burla y desprécio de ellas. Tambien se usaba contra el aojo, quando se alababa, ò se miraba con atencion alguna cosa, y es comun entre los Moros, los quales haciendo la higa dicen: *Xampza febabinak*, que se interpreta Cinco en tu ojo. De aqui ha quedado el abuso entre nosotros de hacer la higa, assi quando queremos despreciar à alguna persona, como quando por lisonja queremos celebrar su hermosúra" (*Aut.*).

del trabajo deste día:
"Número uno, Alcaicería,
embuste de casamiento".

Las doncellas más sesudas
me creen cualquier disparate
como en casamiento trate,
y no lo escupen las viudas.

"En Cal★[36] de Bayona, el pelo Calle
a una vieja he de enrubiar,
y en Cal de Francos, quitar
unas pecas y un recelo".

Aquesto el gasto ordinario
me dará; muy pobre estoy
de enredos, pues me hallo[37] hoy
sin embuste extraordinario.[38]

Ya del amor el comercio
está poco liberal;
el amante más leal
no da un cuarto por un tercio.[39]

Mas yo inventé una quimera
que es la que más me ha valido;
y es que yo misma he fingido
que soy tan grande hechicera,

que sé el punto donde estriba
la fortuna, y que comprehendo★[40] comprendo
la astrología, mintiendo
aun de las tejas arriba.

Es esto de las estrellas
el más seguro mentir,
pues ninguno puede[41] ir
a preguntárselo a ellas.

Por mentir a lo gitano,

---

[36] *Cal*—"Lo mismo que Calle abreviada la pronunciación. Usase en algunas partes de Andalucía, especialmente en Sevilla, donde dicen Cal de Génova, Cal de Francos, &c" (*Aut.*).

[37] Dilefa entre "hallo" y "hoy".

[38] Sinéresis en "extraordinario".

[39] No da ni una moneda sin importancia por una tercera.

[40] Sinéresis de "comprehendo".

[41] Dialefa entre "puede" e "ir".

a todos la mano tomo,
y me voy por ella, como
por la palma de la mano.[42]
Finjo lo que hace un ausente,
que haré amar en dos instantes;
y esto lo creen los amantes,
que son bonísima gente;
siendo así, que es cosa rara,
que ni echar las habas sé,[43]
pues no ha habido vieja que
no lo sepa.
[VOZ] Para, para. *Dentro.*

Sale ANTONIA.

ANTONIA ¡Ah de casa!
CELESTINA Mi Antoñica,
¿qué se ofrece por acá?
ANTONIA Mi señora es la que está
a la puerta, y te suplica
mi amor que en cierto cuidado,
que viene a comunicar,
con la fineza has* de obrar hayas
que sabes.
CELESTINA Es excusado
el ruego; di a su merced[44]
que entre luego.
ANTONIA Voy volando. *Vase.*
CELESTINA No se va esto mal trazando:
a esta moza acomodé
en casa desta señora
con título de sobrina,
porque es bonita y ladina;
y un galán, que a su ama adora,

---

[42] *Como por la "palma" de la mano*—"Modo de hablar, con que se significa la facilidad de executar ò conseguir alguna cosa" (*Aut.*).

[43] *Echar las habas*—"Phrase con que se explica que algun Hechicéro se aparta à hacer sus conjúros, hechizos ò sortilégios" (*Aut.*).

[44] Como se verifica según la rima de la redondilla, no se pronuncia la "d" de "merced".

me la hizo echar por espía
en su casa, y como ha sido
también de las que han creído
mi fingida hechicería,
yo apuesto que su ama ahora
venirme a ver determina
por mágica o adivina.

Sale[n] DOÑA ANA y ANTONIA.

DOÑA ANA ¿Celestina?
CELESTINA Mi señora,
¿esta casa tan feliz?
DOÑA ANA No me puedo detener,
porque de Granada ayer
mi prima doña Beatriz[45]
llegó, con que a recibilla★ recibirla
a una quinta, en que está, voy;
pues mi padre quiere que hoy
entre con ella en Sevilla;
mas viendo que en el camino
y apartada del lugar
tu casa está, quise entrar
a verte, porque imagino
que tú el alivio has de ser
de un cuidado, de un pesar,
que no le sabré explicar,
aunque lo sé padecer.
Yo sé que la primacía
tienes de cuantos ha habido
que la ciencia han aprehendido★[46] aprendido
de magia y astrología;
y si acaso haces por mí
lo que espero, te prometo
que galardón y secreto
tengas.

[45] De aquí en adelante hay sinéresis en "Beatriz". También es uso común del siglo XVII, como se ve en *La dama duende* de Calderón, donde "Beatriz" se da como vocabo bisilábico.

[46] Sinéresis en "aprehendido".

CELESTINA No más, que por ti,
hasta donde mi experiencia
llegare, pienso probar.
DOÑA ANA Yo sé lo que puede obrar,
Celestina, tu gran ciencia,
y ésta a todos es notoria.
CELESTINA Los buenos siempre honran mucho.
DOÑA ANA Atiende, pues.
CELESTINA Ya te escucho;
comienza tu amarga historia.
DOÑA ANA De un amante di atención
a las ansias amorosas.
CELESTINA Poco a poco, que estas cosas
piden gran cuenta y razón.
DOÑA ANA De un amante mi beldad
a las quejas dio atención,
y halléme una inclinación,
con el traje de piedad;
vuelto el desdén en clemencia,
al punto el amor triunfó,
porque el desdén, cuando huyó,
llamó a la correspondencia;
viéndose favorecido
mi amante . . .
CELESTINA ¿Qué? ¿Se entibió?
DOÑA ANA Al contrario, antes quedó
más constante y más rendido;
si te cuento los excesos
de su amor, te admirará.
CELESTINA Desde Macías[47] acá
no se hallará un hombre desos.
DOÑA ANA Con el aura del favor
y con la fuerza del trato,
sulcábamos* el mar grato surcábamos
en los piélagos de amor,
cuando en el golfo sereno

[47] *Macías el enamorado*—El amante por antonomasia. Véanse *Porfiar hasta morir* de Lope de Vega y *El español más amante y desgraciado, Macías* de Bances Candamo y otros. Además Larra escribió su *Macías* y la novela *El doncel de don Enrique "el doliente"*.

levantó el cierzo traidor
fiera borrasca.
CELESTINA El amor
tiene de eso mucho y bueno.
DOÑA ANA A este mismo tiempo había,
aunque de mí despreciado,
otro amante, tan cansado,
que más que afecto, porfía
era su amor, pues no fue
bastante mi indignación
a impedir su pretensión.
CELESTINA Mira, muchos sienten que
los desprecios son muy buenos;
a otros enfrían también;
mas cree que esto del desdén
tiene su más y su menos.
DOÑA ANA Tan ciega, tan obstinada
fue su pasión que, por ver
si podía merecer
que le oyese, a una criada
con dádivas granjeó,
que mi ruina vino a ser.
ANTONIA Miren qué infame mujer;
qué poco lo hiciera yo.
DOÑA ANA Una noche infausta*, en fin, infeliz
que esta traidora infïel
estaba hablando con él
por la reja de un jardín,
llegó mi amante, y por ser,
para más desdicha mía,
la parte donde solía
hablar conmigo, a creer
se persuadió sus recelos,
sin preguntar ni inquirir,
que hasta en el no discurrir
son ignorantes los celos;
con que loco y temerario
con su enemigo embistió,
y a poco rato quedó
mal herido su contrario.
Llegando gente al rüido,

fue el que ambos se retirasen
preciso, sin que quedasen
uno de otro conocido.
Viendo el herido ignorada
la mano de quién le hirió,
a pocos días pasó,
de despechado, a Granada.
Mi amante con tal certeza
creyó traición en mi fe,
que, sin verme más, se fue
a Flandes. Desde aquí empieza
mi ruego contigo.

CELESTINA Di.

DOÑA ANA Es que tú me has de saber
si le he de volver a ver,
si allí se acuerda de mí,
o si ya su voluntad
se ha entibiado con la ausencia.

CELESTINA Negocio es, en mi conciencia,
que tiene dificultad;
mas yo pienso echar el resto
en esta ocasión por ti.

DOÑA ANA No lo perderás.

CELESTINA Así
que se me olvidaba[48] esto,
¿el nombre?

DOÑA ANA Don Juan de Lara
se llama.

CELESTINA Puede importar.

DOÑA ANA Y con quien tuvo el pesar
fue don Diego de Guevara.

CELESTINA Está bien.

DOÑA ANA ¿Cuándo podré
volver a verte?

CELESTINA Estas cosas,
aunque son dificultosas,
cuando vuelvas yo estaré
en tu casa, con pretexto

[48] Dialefa entre "olvidada" y "esto".

de vender las bujerías
que son del uso estos días.
DOÑA ANA ¡Grande es tu saber!
CELESTINA Mas esto
sólo quede entre las dos.
DOÑA ANA De mi parte te prometo
la paga con el secreto.
CELESTINA Pues adiós, señora.
DOÑA ANA Adiós.
CELESTINA ([*Aparte*] ¡Ay tan graciosa inocente!)
¿Oyes, te acuerdas, o no,
qué día y hora sucedió?
DOÑA ANA El día de San Clemente,[49]
que no lo he olvidado, en fe
de que el más festivo día
de Sevilla, su alegría
mi mayor tristeza fue.[50]
CELESTINA ¿Y la[51] hora?
DOÑA ANA Entre una y dos
de la noche.
CELESTINA Bien está.

Aparte a ANTONIA.

CELESTINA ([*Aparte*] ¿Hablaste a don Diego?)
ANTONIA ([*Aparte*] Ya.)
DOÑA ANA Adiós, Celestina.
CELESTINA Adiós.

Vanse DOÑA ANA *y* ANTONIA.

CELESTINA Dejen ahora que me ría
de aquesta sinceridad;
miren la dificultad
que tiene esta hechicería.

---

[49] El tercer sucesor de San Pedro, cuya fiesta se celebra el 23 de noviembre.
[50] San Clemente es el patrón de Sevilla.
[51] Dilefa entre "la" y "hora" o entre "hora" y "Entre".

De aquél que en Flandes está
el saber lo que hace trata.
Pues ven acá, mentecata,
si, a saber lo que hace allá,
a Flandes no puedes ir,
ni te es posible el saber,
¿no te es preciso creer
lo que yo quiera decir?
Entre mis embustes grandes
este Flandes se inventó,
aunque, para mentir yo,
lo mismo es aquí que en Flandes.
Diréle, por cosa cierta,
que su galán sí no está,
y que presto le verá . . .
mas llamaron a la puerta. *Llaman.*
¿Quién llama? [*romances*]

Sale MUÑOZ.

MUÑOZ Mi Celestina.
CELESTINA Mi Muñoz, ¡en esta casa
tanta dicha! ¡Qué te veo
después de ausencia tan larga!
¿Adónde has estado?
MUÑOZ A Flandes
pasé con don Juan de Lara,
mi señor.
CELESTINA Vuelve a decir,
¿cómo tu señor se llama?
MUÑOZ Don Juan de Lara.
CELESTINA ([*Aparte*] ¿Si fuera
el ausente de doña Ana
el tal don Juan?)
MUÑOZ Y a la puerta
está, que, en cierta demanda
amorosa, quiso que
contigo le apadrinara,
habiéndole dicho yo
nuestra amistad y tu maña
en estas cosas.

CELESTINA Y ¿qué es
el negocio?
MUÑOZ Cierta dama
que vio en una quinta . . . pero,
puesto que a la puerta aguarda,
él te lo dirá mejor;
y mira que por él hagas
lo que a mi amistad le debes.
Voy a llamarle. *Vase.*
CELESTINA ¡Qué rara
ocasión se me ha ofrecido!
Un embuste se me fragua*, idea
que yo . . . pero ello dirá.

Sale[n] DON JUAN, TACON y MUÑOZ.

CELESTINA Mi señor don Juan de Lara,
vos seáis muy bien venido.
DON JUAN Hasta que por mí te hablara
Muñoz, como forastero,
no quise entrar en tu casa;
pero él tiene en tu amistad
tan segura confianza
que ha asegurado la mía,
creyendo que por mí hagas
una fineza de que
tendrás segura la paga
como el agradecimiento.
CELESTINA Aunque la amistad faltara
de Muñoz, vuestra persona
por recomendación basta;
y ¿tú no me hablas, Tacón?
TACON Usté a su negocio vaya,
que los dos no nos tiramos.
CELESTINA ¿Todavía estás de mala
conmigo?
DON JUAN ¿Que siempre seas
majadero?
TACON Pese a mi alma,
¿pues no he de estar mal con quien
me quitó la más bizarra

moza que empuñó barreños* lavabos
y que manejó aljofainas*? vasijas
La morena de más cielos
era que vió esta comarca;
mas luego que me quitaron
el dinero, esta borracha
la traspuso, y me dejó
sin mi morena y sin blanca.[52]
DON JUAN Calla, loco; Celestina,
yo tengo noticias raras
de tu grande habilidad
y cuánto con ella tratas
de hacer gusto a los amigos.
CELESTINA Eso sí tengo, a Dios gracias.
DON JUAN Sabe que yo de Sevilla
me ausenté . . .
CELESTINA Por una dama
y unos celos.
DON JUAN Pues ¿de qué
puedes tú saberlo?
CELESTINA Pasa
adelante, que hasta ahora
aun no sabes con quién hablas.
TACON ¿Diga usted ahora[53] que no es
hechicera?
DON JUAN Necio, calla.
Muñoz, llévale allá fuera.
MUÑOZ Vamos.
TACON De muy buena gana
me iré, sólo por no ver
esa maldidta endiablada,
cara a cara tutelar,
carota y carantamaula.*[54] caradura y fea
DON JUAN Es verdad que cierta noche . . .
CELESTINA Entre una y dos, la desgracia

---

[52] Juego de palabras basado en una dilogía: *Blanca* quiere decir moneda además de una mujer blanca.

[53] Sinéresis en "ahora".

[54] *Carota*—caradura; desvergonzada. *Carantamaula*—careta de cartón, de aspecto horrible y feo.

te sucedió de encontrar
tu enemigo con tu dama,
y él quedó herido.

DON JUAN ¿De dónde
has tenido tan extrañas
noticias?

CELESTINA Pasa adelante,
que aun no sabes con quién hablas.

DON JUAN Este suceso . . .

CELESTINA Que fue,
para mayor circunstancia,
aquel celebrado día
en que Sevilla ganada
hace fiesta a San Clemente.

DON JUAN ¡Vive Dios, que harás que vaya
creyendo . . . !

CELESTINA Pasa adelante,
que esto ha sido sólo maña
por que* de mí fíes que — para que
sabré hacer lo que me mandas.

DON JUAN No quiero ahora[55] discurrir
de tus noticias la causa,
y así, voy a lo que importa.
En esta última jornada,
antes de entrar en Sevilla,
hallé imitando a Dïana
una hermosa cazadora,
a cuya belleza rara
rendí la vida, por que* — porque
en su beldad soberana,
desde el adorarla al verla,
no puso el amor distancia.

CELESTINA Y ¿no supiste quién era?

DON JUAN Eso de tu vigilancia
saber espero.

CELESTINA ¿Ni el nombre
siquiera?

DON JUAN Yo no sé nada

[55] Sinéresis en “ahora”.

más que amarla.

CELESTINA Buen despacho
tenemos con sólo amarla,
cuando della no sabemos
quién es, ni cómo se llama
ni dónde vive.

DON JUAN Esto sólo
puedo decir: ella estaba
en una quinta que está
media legua de Trïana.

CELESTINA ([*Aparte.*] Si fuera estotra la prima
que va a llevar a su casa
doña Ana, corrieran hoy
mis embustes con bonanza.)

DON JUAN ¿Qué dices? ¿Qué me respondes?

CELESTINA Que el negocio es de importancia
y de los irregulares;
pero buenas esperanzas,
que quizás sabrás, no sólo
quién es y cómo se llama,
pero dónde la hallarás,
para verla y para hablarla;
esto quiere más espacio,
y hoy no puedo estar en casa,
por ir a la de don Luis
de Ribera, que palabra
di de llevar a una[56] hija,
que tiene, ciertas alhajas
que son del uso estos días.

DON JUAN ([*Aparte*] Mejor dirás a una ingrata,
pues la[57] hija de don Luis
fue de mi ausencia la causa.)

CELESTINA ¿Qué te suspende?

DON JUAN He sentido
la ocasión con que dilatas,
por ir a otros intereses,
el consuelo de mis ansias.

---

[56] Dialefa entre "una" e "hija".

[57] Dialefa entre "la" e "hija".

Bien que, por que* ellas no pierdan — para que
tiempo y tú donde has de ir vayas,
tras ti iré donde podremos
volver a vernos, a causa
de que yo para don Luis
traigo desde Flandes cartas
de un sobrino, a quien no pude
excusar el acetarlas*; — aceptarlas
que no había de decirle,
siendo su prima mi dama,
la razón que yo tenía
para no entrar en su casa.
Con que, como dije, allá
nos veremos.

CELESTINA Como vayas
tú allá, podrá ser . . .

DON JUAN Prosigue.

CELESTINA . . . que te cumpla mi palabra
de saber lo que deseas,
y aun, si el magín* no me engaña, — imaginación
que la veas, por lo menos.

DON JUAN Prometes con tal confianza
en cosa tan imposible,
como estar ella distancia
de Sevilla y no saber
quién es y cómo se llama,
que tu habilidad no sé
a qué lo atribuya.

CELESINA Calla,
que tú me conocerás,
y adiós, porque allá me aguardan;
y, para tu dependencia,
es menester que antes haga
unas ciertas diligencias.

DON JUAN Estos escudos, no paga
son, sino cariño.

CELESTINA Eso es
correrme, y no los tomara,
a no venir de tu mano.

DON JUAN Adiós.

CELESTINA Adiós.

Dentro ruido de cuchilladas.

DON DIEGO La ventaja *Dentro.*
no os ha de valer, cobardes.
DON JUAN A la puerta de tu casa
hay cuchilladas.
CELESTINA Pues si es
pendencia, allá se las hayan,
que, teniendo yo los oros,
no he menester las espadas.[58]
DON JUAN Adiós, hasta luego. *Vase.*
CELESTINA Adiós.
Un hechizo se me traza
tan prohibido que tiene
cuatro palmos más de marca.[59] *Vase.*

CUADRO III

Sale DON DIEGO riñendo con algunos.

DON DIEGO Cobardes, vuestra osadía
habéis de ver castigada,
aunque estoy solo.
UNO Eso ahora
lo veremos.

Sale DON JUAN.

DON JUAN Tan villana
acción merece el castigo
que veréis.
OTRO Antes que vaya
llegando más gente, huyamos. *[Vanse.]*
DON JUAN ¿Así volvéis las espaldas?

---

[58] "Oros" y "espadas" se refieren a la baraja española.

[59] *Palmo*—una medida. *De mas de "marca" ù de "marca" mayor*—"Phrase con que se explica que alguna cosa es excessiva en su linea, y passa y sobrepuja à lo justo y razonáble" (*Aut.*).

Mas ¿cuándo no son cobardes
los que riñen con ventaja?
DON DIEGO Aunque huyáis, he de seguiros.
DON JUAN. No los sigáis, pues que basta
que vuestro valor los ponga
en fuga.
DON DIEGO Si vuestra espada
a mi lado no estuviera,
siendo tanta la ventaja,
bien conozco que mi vida
corriera riesgo; y pues tanta
es mi obligación, merezca
saber quién sois, que es villana
acción, viendo el beneficio,
tener del dueño ignorancia.
DON JUAN Para que veáis[60] cuánto estimo
vuestra atención, sólo a causa
de que me podáis mandar
en todo lo que yo valga,
haré lo que me pedís:
mi nombre es don Juan de Lara;
sepa yo el vuestro, y también
me decid qué fue la causa
deste disgusto.
DON DIEGO Mi nombre
es don Diego de Guevara,
para seviros, y el lance
que visteis fue que, en la casa
del juego, sobre una suerte
tuve no sé qué palabras
anoche, y hoy que salí
a pasearme a Trïana,
queriendo el interesado
tomar segura venganza,
acompañado de esotros,
me siguió; y si vuestra espada
a mi lado no estuviera,
yo imagino que lograra

[60] Sinéresis en "veáis".

su intención; y permitidme
que lo repita, pues paga
en parte ya el beneficio
quien le confiesa.

Sale TACON.

TACON — El que anda
a caza de amos, es peor[61]
que andar a caza de gangas.
DON JUAN — Ven acá, loco.

Sale MUÑOZ.

MUÑOZ — ¡Señor!
No imaginé que te hallara.
DON JUAN — ¿Dónde habéis estado?
TACON — Al punto
que escuchamos las espadas,
fuimos a esgrimir las copas,
que es la pendencia más sana.
DON JUAN — Hicisteis como crïados.
DON DIEGO — Ellos hacen poca falta
donde está vuestro valor.
MUÑOZ — Mas ahora, viendo que anda
la justicia en estos barrios,
te buscamos por que* vayas — para que
a descansar, pues ya es de noche.
DON JUAN — Venid, que hasta vuestra casa
os he de ir acompañando.
DON DIEGO — Yo acetaré*, si es que a honrarla — aceptaré
queréis ir.
DON JUAN — Vuestra fineza
no dudéis que la acetara,
a no tener esta noche
negocio tan de importancia,
que faltar a él no es posible.
DON DIEGO — No obstante, yo os porfïara,

[61] Sinéresis en "peor".

a no parecerme indigna
a tal huésped la posada,
pues casi soy forastero
como vos, pues de Granada
poco ha que llegué a Sevilla;
y pues que no os sirvo en nada,
adiós, que en la ocupación
el que no sirve, embaraza.

DON JUAN Esperad.

DON DIEGO Yo os buscaré.
([*Aparte*] A la criada de doña Ana
iré a hablar por el jardín.) *Vase.*

MUÑOZ ¿Quién es éste?

DON JUAN Tan extrañas
son, al entrar en Sevilla,
las cosas que por mí pasan,
que aun yo mismo las ignoro.
Vamos, pues, donde me aguarda
Celestina.

TACON Yo recelo
en los embustes que traza,
que ha de ser peor[62] tu salida,
con ser tan mala tu entrada. *Vanse.*

CUADRO IV

Salen DOÑA ANA, DOÑA BEATRIZ, DON LUIS, ANTONIA y INES.

DON LUIS Sobrina, aunque el hospedaje [*romances*]
no es conforme a los deseos,
súplalo el afecto, pues
no hay límite en el afecto.
Y ahora, dadme licencia,
que embarazaros no quiero,
que es justo que descanséis;
y también, porque supuesto

[62] Sinéresis en "peor". Véase v. 963.

que a Cádiz ha de ir mi hermano,
irle acompañando quiero,
hasta salir de Sevilla.

DOÑA BEATRIZ Vos, en todo, tan atento
sois que yo no hallo palabras,
señor, para agradeceros
los favores que me hacéis.

DON LUIS Hija, a tu cuidado dejo
la asistencia de tu prima. *Vase.*

DOÑA ANA Prima, si al merecimiento
se ha de medir el cuidado,
mal podré yo del empeño
sacar a mi padre.

DOÑA BEATRIZ Deja,
doña Ana, los cumplimientos,
que desconfiaré de ti
si perseveras en ellos;
y te he menester tan mía
que tú el alivio, el remedio
has de ser de unos pesares
que, aunque caben en el pecho,
en la explicación no caben;
pues aun niegan el aliento
a la voz, por ser la voz
al referirlos consuelo.

DOÑA ANA Pues para que veas, Beatriz,[63]
que ya en parte te obedezco
y te trato con llaneza,
que te recojas, te ruego,
y te alivies de ese traje,
que también contigo tengo
que comunicar pesares;
quizá las dos hallaremos
en referir nuestras penas
alivio, si no remedio.
Antonia, lleva a mi prima
a su cuarto, y vuelve presto,
que te he menester.

---

[63] Sinéresis en "veas" y "Beatriz". Véase v. 937.

DOÑA BEATRIZ Pues mira
que allá aguardando te quedo.
DOÑA ANA Véte, pues, que por servirte
sólo a ti por ti te dejo. *Vase.*
DOÑA BEATRIZ Pues mira que espero. Inés
ven conmigo. *Vase.*
ANTONIA Las dos hemos
de ser muy grandes amigas,
señora Inés.
INES Yo me alegro
de tener tal compañera;
que el servir juntas, es cierto
que engendra grande cariño.
ANTONIA Y ése será más estrecho.
INES ¿Cuándo?
ANTONIA Cuando a nuestras amas
vendamos y murmuremos. *Va[n]se.*

CUADRO V

Sale DOÑA ANA.

DOÑA ANA Mucho tarda Celestina,
y si no viniere presto,
la asistencia de Beatriz[64]
me ha de embarazar.

Sale CELESTINA.

CELESTINA *Laus Deo.*
DOÑA ANA Ya desconfiaba de ti.
CELESTINA Mucho me agravias en eso;
no soy yo mujer que falto
jamás a lo que prometo.
DOÑA ANA Pues dime, ¿qué has alcanzado
en si es que hace algún acuerdo

---

[64] Sinéresis en "Beatriz".

don Juan de mí, y si será
verdad que he de verle presto?

CELESTINA ([*Aparte*] Diréla que sí, que nada
en que no suceda pierdo,
y gano[65] lo que ha de darme
si su esperanza entretengo.)
[*A ella*] Mira, si me sale bien
un hervidillo que dejo
sazonado, que atractivo
es de ausentes, ten por cierto . . .

DOÑA ANA Di.

CELESTINA . . . que presto le verás.

DOÑA ANA Esto es agradecimiento,
no paga; este anillo toma.

Dale una sortija.

CELESTINA No hay para qué.

DOÑA ANA Y dime . . . pero
¿llaman a la puerta?

CELESTINA Sí.

DOÑA ANA Pues en el recibimiento
sin una crïada estamos,
responder yo misma intento.
¿Quién es?

Sale DON JUAN.[66]

DON JUAN Quien buscando viene . . .
([*Aparte*] Mas doña Ana es la que veo.
¡Qué en el primer paso[67] hubo
de ser azar el encuentro!)

DOÑA ANA ¿A quién. . . ? ([*Aparte*] Mas ¿qué es lo que miro?
Don Juan es, ¡valedme, cielos!

---

[65] En todas las ediciones se dice "pierdo" menos en TS, a la cual sigo aquí.

[66] Vv. 1093–1146 tienen mucho en común con el final del Acto II de *El astrólogo fingido* de Calderón de la Barca.

[67] Dialefa entre "paso" y "hubo".

Que si hasta aquí fue de amor,
ya es de temor el afecto.)

DON JUAN
No te asustes de mirarme,
fiera ingrata, presumiendo
que vengo por ti a tu casa,
que no eres tú por quien vengo;
violento y forzado, a causa
de un mandato que obedezco,
vengo a . . .

DOÑA ANA
No prosigas, ya
sé que forzado y violento
vienes; y pues yo, al mirarte,
turbada y confusa tiemblo,
véte en paz; no, no te acerques,
que, aunque sin ti mi deseo
me alentaba, no me cabe
ya el corazón en el pecho.

CELESTINA
([*Aparte*] ¡Por el siglo de mi abuela,
qué este don Juan es el mesmo
que ofrecí traer[68] a doña Ana![69]
Ven aquí cómo este enredo
se me ha hecho sin sentir.)

DON JUAN
Ay ingrata, como es cierto
que el que ofende ve con susto,
con sobresalto y con miedo
la cara del ofendido.

DOÑA ANA
No es eso, don Juan, no es eso,
sino. . . —mas ¡no puedo hablar!—
sino. . . —¡ni aun alentar puedo!—
sino que haberme valido
del encanto te confieso;
mas no, como tú imaginas,
mi traición, sino mi afecto
buscó medio tan indigno,
porque el amor, como es ciego,

[68] Sinéresis en "traer".

[69] A la luz de vv. 865–880, este aparte y exclamación son superfluos como revelación porque ya sabe Celestina que don Juan era galán de doña Ana. Sin embargo, como expresión espontánea de regocijo al ver que sus embustes van saliendo bien, son dramáticamente expresivos.

para conseguir sus fines,
nunca repara en los medios.
Mi amor, pues . . . —mas ¡ay de mí,
que aun a respirar no acierto!—
Vuélvete, don Juan.

DON JUAN Tirana,
no entiendo tus fingimientos;
y vive Dios, que has de oír
toda la razon que tengo,
y que has de ver . . .

DOÑA ANA No te acerques,
que el corazón, el aliento,
la acción, la vida, la voz
desfallecen . . . ¡Piedad, cielos!
Inés, Antonia, Beatriz,[70]
favorecedme. *Vase.*

DON JUAN ¿Qué es esto,
mujer? ¿Qué encanto es aquéste?
Cuando a ver a la que quiero
me traes,[71] ¿me pones delante
la que me ofende?[72]

CELESTINA A ese duelo
presto he de satisfacerte.

DOÑA ANA Prima, Beatriz.[73] *Dentro.*

Sale DOÑA BEATRIZ por la otra parte.

DOÑA BEATRIZ ¿Qué es aquesto?
¿Qué accidente . . . ? Mas ¡qué miro!

DON JUAN ¡Cielos! ¿Qué es esto que veo?

CELESTINA ([*Aparte*] ¿Si es aquésta la que quiere?)

DON JUAN Mujer, toda eres portentos.

DOÑA BEATRIZ ¡Sí es encanto del sentido!

DON JUAN ¡Sí es ilusión del deseo!

---

[70] Sinéresis en "Beatriz".

[71] Sinéresis en "traes".

[72] Hay que recordar que, cuando don Juan comenzó a cortejar a doña Ana, ella vivía entonces en la casa de su tío (vv. 121–26).

[73] Sinéresis en "Beatriz".

Encanto de mi albedrío,
que en ninguna ocasión puedo
decir mejor que no[74] hay
encanto como lo bello,
dime, ¿qué superior causa
me trae a ver tus reflejos
segunda vez, para que
segunda vez quede ciego?

DOÑA BEATRIZ Hombre, ilusión o fantasma,
que, a pesar de mi despecho,
me sigue más tu osadía
que tu pasión, pues es cierto
que no cabe en amor noble
lo vil del atrevimiento,
¿qué intentas?

DON JUAN Sólo que sepas
que es tan contrario mi afecto,
que primero adoración
que voluntad fue en el pecho,
sin que pise la esperanza
el umbral del pensamiento,
y así

DOÑA BEATRIZ No más, no prosigas,
que ya es faltar al respecto
de mi decoro el oírte.

DON JUAN Si me atiendes . . .

DONA BEATRIZ No te atiendo.

DON JUAN . . . vieras . . .

DOÑA BEATRIZ ¿Qué tengo de ver?

DON JUAN . . . mi disculpa . . .

DOÑA BEATRIZ No la quiero.

DON JUAN . . . porque mi amor . . .

DOÑA BEATRIZ Es delito.

DON JUAN . . . mi fineza . . .

DOÑA BEATRIZ Atrevimiento.

DON JUAN . . . si me escuchas.

DOÑA BEATRIZ Desta suerte
haz que te responda el viento. *Vase.*

---

[74] Dialefa entre "no" y "hay".

DON JUAN Sabré yo seguirte.
CELESTINA Espera,
no más, bueno está lo bueno;
vaya usted ahora[75] con Dios,
que mañana nos veremos,
pues ya cumplí mi palabra.
DON JUAN Tan absorto voy que creo
lo mismo que estoy dudando;
amor, ¿qué encantos son éstos?
CELESTINA Deja ahora exclamaciones,
pues en mí hallarás consuelos,
que soy mujer tan insigne,
que en los siglos venideros
de mí ha de decir la fama
esto, y estotro y aquello.[76]

---

[75] Sinéresis en "ahora".
[76] Hay dos dialefas en este verso.

SEGUNDA JORNADA

Cuadro I

Sale[n] DON LUIS y DOÑA ANA.

DON LUIS ¿Te has despedido, doña Ana, [*romances*]
de tu tío?
DOÑA ANA Por más señas,
que al despedirse me dio
esta joya.
DON LUIS Esas son muestras
de la voluntad que siempre
te ha tenido; y pues se ausenta
a Cádiz a conclüir
de flota mis dependencias*, negocios
y, hasta salir de Sevilla,
irle acompañando es fuerza;
aunque yo volveré presto,
te ruego, hija, que gran cuenta
tengas con tu casa, que
quizá importará.
DOÑA ANA Es tan nueva
esa prevención en ti
que me pones en sospecha
de que . . .
DON LUIS No sospeches nada,
que esta prevención es cuerda.
([*Aparte*] ¡Qué mal se oculta un pesar!
Anoche por una reja
del jardín vi hablar a un hombre,
que se ausentó con tal priesa
al verme, que no me fue
posible seguirle. ¡Ah fiera
ley del honor!)
DOÑA ANA El mirarte

tan suspenso me da muestras,
señor, que algún gran cuidado
te aflige, y que no merezca
el saberlo yo me admira.

DON LUIS
([*Aparte*] ¡Mal el corazón se esfuerza!)
Yo,[1] hija, no tengo nada
que sentir, adiós te queda,
que yo presto volveré.
([*Aparte*] Paciencia, cielos, paciencia,
hasta averiguar mejor
mi mal, pues sólo remedian
males de honor el silencio,
el cuidado y la prudencia.) *Vase.*

DOÑA ANA
¡Qué misterioso mi padre
me ha hablado! No sé qué sea
esta novedad. ¡Antonia!

Sale ANTONIA.

ANTONIA
¿Señora?

DOÑA ANA
Di, ¿en la asistencia
de los huéspedes ha habido
alguna falta?

ANTONIA
Que sepa
yo, no ha[2] habido ninguna,
por cuidado u diligencia;
pero ¿por qué lo preguntas?

DOÑA ANA
Porque mi padre, que tenga
gran cuidado con la casa,
con palabras muy severas,
me ha mandado.

ANTONIA
([*Aparte*] Esto, sin duda,
es que anoche por la reja
hablar me vio con don Diego.)
Quizá será impertinencia
de mi señor.

DOÑA ANA
¿Y tu tía?

---

[1] Dialefa entre "yo" e "hija".
[2] Dialefa entre "ha" y "habido".

ANTONIA Desde anoche compañera[3]
la tengo en mi cuarto.
DOÑA ANA ¿Qué hace
mi prima?
ANTONIA Ella la respuesta
te dará, pues que ya sale.
([*Aparte*] Voy a disponer que venga
don Diego a hablar a mi[4] ama,
fingiendo alguna cautela
como se lo prometí:
¡ay lealtad,[5] lo que me cuestas!) *[Vase.]*

Sale DOÑA BEATRIZ.

DOÑA BEATRIZ ¡Prima!
DOÑA ANA ¡Beatriz![6]
DOÑA BEATRIZ Esperando
a que tu padre se fuera
he estado, para venir
a verte, que ya que cuenta
me has dado de tus pesares
y de tu amor, yo quisiera
que tú aliviases los míos
con tu atención, que, aunque sienta
referir penas, se alivian
comunicadas las penas.
DOÑA ANA Pues que yo te he descubierto
mi pecho, cree que en él tengas
lástima para sentirlas
y piedad para atenderlas.
DOÑA BEATRIZ Pues antes que mis pesares
te repita, el darte cuenta
es preciso de un cuidado,
que es muy posible que pueda,

---

[3] Para los vv. 1258–1414, sigo 1694 por faltar dos páginas en el microfilme de 1681 que manejo.

[4] Dialefa entre "mi" y "ama".

[5] Sinéresis en "lealtad".

[6] Sinéresis en "Beatriz".

sin ser culpa de las dos,
que de las dos riesgo sea.
Sabe que, estando en la quinta,
salí a caza a la ribera
de Guadalquivir, y un hombre
forastero con tal tema
me dio en seguir, que me fue
precisa la diligencia
de retirarme, por verme
libre dél; pero fue[7] esta
diligencia inútil, pues
anoche fue de manera
su atrevimiento que entró
en tu casa, y de su necia
pasión volvió a repetirme
las lisonjas que en mi ofensa
fueron; y porque es posible
que determinado vuelva
otra vez, quiero avisarte,
mirando cuánto se arriesga
mi honor y el tuyo.

DOÑA ANA Si acaso
volviere, a mi cargo deja
castigar su atrevimiento.

DOÑA BEATRIZ Pues ahora, para que veas[8]
adónde llegan de amor
las no entendidas cautelas,
cuando en las selvas del Betis
quiere el amor que aborrezca,
fue porque ya su dominio
reconocí en otras selvas.
Ya sabes que, aunque en Sevilla
nací, desde mi edad tierna
me crié en Granada,[9] a causa
de tener mi padre en ella
de pleitos y pretensiones

---

[7] Dialefa entre "fue" y "esta".
[8] Hay sinéresis en "ahora" y en "veas".
[9] Dialefa entre "Granada" y "a".

las precisas dependencias.
Libre del amor vivía,
tan sin recelar sus flechas,
tan sin temor de sus plumas,
que en mí los desprecios eran
naturaleza, por que*, porque
si no son naturaleza,
tienen visos de favores
los desdenes que se afectan.
Tan dueño de mi albedrío
vivía que las violencias
del amor —vuelvo a decir—
despreciaba. ¡Oh cuánto yerra
quien no recela las iras
de deidad que hiere y vuela!*, Cupido
que, a un enemigo con alas,
ni aun la fuga es resistencia.
Dígalo yo, pues un día,
cuando el alba mal despierta
empezó a pintar las flores
para borrar las estrellas,[10]
saliendo a caza, ejercicio
a que nací de manera
inclinada que trocaba,
por la inquietud de las selvas,
las delicias de la corte,
al penetrar la maleza
de un bosque, me hallé empeñada
con una cerdosa fiera* jabalí
que, irracional Mongibelo*, volcán
por la vista llamas flecha,
humo en alientos respira,
y mares de espuma nieva
por el bruñido marfil,
con que fue encendida[11] Etna* volcán
con humo, llamas y nieve

[10] Véase v. 282 de *El amor más desgraciado, Céfalo y Pocris* de Salazar.
[11] Dialefa entre "encendida" y "Etna".

en aliento, vista y presas*.[12] colmillos
De sus indómitas iras
mal eximirse pudiera
mi vida, si al mismo tiempo
no penetrara la selva
un cazador caballero
que de tal suerte se empeña
por mi riesgo que, sacando
la cuchilla, con la fiera
intrépidamente osado
embistió, con tal violencia
que a repetidas heridas
cedió el bruto su fiereza,
por muchas bocas vertiendo
la vida en purpúrea*[13] envuelta. sangre
Mi agradecimiento causa
fue de que no mal le oyera
no sé qué cortesanías,
tan rendidas, tan atentas,
que no hallaron mis desdenes
razón para su defensa.
¿Quién creerá que, en parecidos
trances de montes y fieras,
en el uno obligue el uno,
y en el otro el otro ofenda?
En fin, para no cansarte,
el acaso de la selva
pasó en la corte a cuidado,
pues su atención, su asistencia,
como mi agradecimiento
las alentaba, fue fuerza,
a pesar de mis rigores,
que mis rigores cedieran;
que desprecia tibia quien
agradecida desprecia.
Mas, en fin, penas y glorias
de amor están tan expuestas

---

[12] Ejemplo de la técnica estilística llamada "diseminación-recolección".
[13] Sinéresis en "purpúrea".

a sus mundanzas, que solos
instantes las diferencian.
Pues mi amante a breve tiempo
le fue precisa la ausencia
de Granada, por llamarle
a forzosas dependencias
sus deudos*, y aunque un alivio parientes
en este caso pudiera
tener, pues vino a Sevilla,
poco o nada se remedia
con hallarle, pues mi padre
casarme en Cádiz intenta,
a pesar de mi albedrío.
¡Ah tirana ley severa
del honor! ¡Ah duro yugo
en que padece violencia
no menos que un alma!

DOÑA ANA No
te aflijas de esa manera,
que puede ser que se[14] halle
remedio a tu mal; da cuenta
a tu amante del pesar
en que te hallas.

DOÑA BEATRIZ Aunque fuera
cierto el hallarle en Sevilla,
¿no ves que la diligencia
de buscarle es muy difícil
para mí?

DOÑA ANA A mi cargo deja
aquesa dificultad.

DOÑA BEATRIZ Mucho debo a tu fineza.

DOÑA ANA Esta en mí es obligación,
y ahora,[15] por que* no se pierda para que
tiempo en buscar a tu amante,
y que tu cuidado sepa . . .
¡Antonia!

---

[14] Dialefa entre "se" y "halle".

[15] Sinéresis en "ahora".

Sale ANTONIA.

ANTONIA ¿Señora?
DOÑA ANA Di
a Celestina que venga.
ANTONIA Ya te obedezco. [*Vase.*]
DOÑA BEATRIZ ¿Quién es
Celestina?
DOÑA ANA Esta es la mesma
mujer que te dije que hizo
que desde Flandes viniera
a verme don Juan de Lara;
mira tú si sabrá[16] ella
buscar ese caballero.
DOÑA BEATRIZ No sé con qué te agradezca,
doña Ana, tantos favores.
DOÑA ANA Ahora cumplimientos deja.

Sale CELESTINA.

CELESTINA Bendiga Dios tanto bueno;
puede ese par de bellezas
poner cátedra de damas.[17]
DOÑA ANA Pues ¿el ser damas es ciencia?
CELESTINA Y tan grande que si, como
aprendieron en Atenas
la docta filosofía,
a ser damas aprendieran,
no habían*[18] de conseguirlo habrían
los siete sabios de Grecia.
DOÑA ANA Graciosa estás, Celestina;
Beatriz una diligencia
tiene que encargarte, y yo,
el que obres con la fineza

[16] Dialefa entre "sabrá" y "ella".

[17] *Poner cátedra*—Hablar en tono magistral, en cuanto a ser damas.

[18] Véase Samuel Gili y Gaya, p. 162 (núm. 124). De ordinario Salazar prefiere la forma -ra del imperfecto de subjuntivo en la apódosis, y nunca usa la forma -ría. Véanse, como ejemplos, vv. 843–46, 928–32, 956–59, 1357–61, 1858–59 y 2190–92.

que tú sabes, te suplico.
DOÑA BEATRIZ Y que en mí la recompensa
será igual al beneficio.
CELESTINA A ser cosa que yo pueda
hacer, de muy buena gana
os serviré.
DOÑA ANA Tú nos dejas
a entrambas agradecidas.
CELESTINA Pues decid la diligencia
que he de hacer, por que* yo diga para que
si puedo o no puedo hacerla;
que yo hablo con claridad:
no, no, llaneza, llaneza,
lisura y verdad en todo,
que primero es mi conciencia;
esto puedo, esto no puedo;
no hay cosa que más me ofenda
en esta vida que ver
una mujer embustera.
DOÑA BEATRIZ Pues lo que has de hacer por mí
no es tan difícil que puedas
excusarte. Mas, ¿llamaron? *Llaman.*
CELESTINA Veré quién es.

Sale TACON.

TACON ¿Que tú seas
con lo primero que encuentro?
No espero que me suceda
cosa buena en todo el día.
DOÑA ANA Tacón, ¿qué venida es ésta?
¿Adónde queda tu[19] amo?
TACON Cierto que entendí que[20] eran
las doña Anas más corteses;
¿bueno es que yo a verte venga
y preguntes por el otro?

---

[19] Dialefa entre "tu" y "amo". Hay que recordar que doña Ana cree que don Juan llegó a su casa por hechizo.

[20] Dialefa entre "que" y "eran".

Mas, pues tanto lo deseas
saber, sabe que llegamos
ayer de Flandes.
DOÑA ANA Espera,
¿ayer de Flandes llegasteis?
TACON Pues ¿qué novedad es ésta
de que uno vuelva a su patria?
DOÑA ANA No sé; pero por la nueva
tan gustosa para mí,
toma esta joya.
CELESTINA Las piedras
se te vuelvan guijarros.
TACON Si aqueso me sucediera,
sobre la joya fundara
mayorazgo en tu cabeza.
Y tú vivas cien mil años,
pero sin llegar a vieja.
DOÑA BEATRIZ ¿Quién es éste?
DOÑA ANA Este es crïado
de don Juan.
TACON Y por más señas*, específicamente
que para subir, aguarda
de tu padre la licencia,
porque le trae unas cartas
de Flandes.
DOÑA ANA Dile que venga,
que yo las recibiré.
TACON Voy a obedecerte.
CELESTINA Muestra,
Tacón, veremos la joya.
TACON Antes ciegues que tal veas. *Vase.*
DOÑA ANA Celestina, ¿qué es aquesto?
CELESTINA ¿Qué ha de ser? ¿Pudo mi ciencia
más alcanzar que saber
la hora en que don Juan viniera,
y en aquel instante mismo
traerle a que tú le veas,
sin que él pudiera eximirse
a una precisa violencia?
DOÑA ANA Digo que tienes razón.
DOÑA BEATRIZ Prima, supuesto que quedas

ahora esperando a don Juan,
danos a las dos licencia
para que a discurrir vamos* vayamos
en estotra diligencia.
DOÑA ANA Ya sabes que siempre sigo
tu gusto.
DOÑA BEATRIZ De tu fineza
está pendiente mi dicha.
CELESTINA De buena parte las cuelgas. *Vanse las dos.*

Sale[n] DON JUAN y TACON.

DON JUAN Pensarás, tirana injusta,
pensarás, hermosa fiera,
ya que el susto se pasó
de que por sombra me tengas,
que de aquel pasado incendio
las no apagadas pavesas,
al aliento de tus ojos,
a ser llama otra vez vuelvan.
Pensarás que, cual incauta,
simple mariposa ciega,
a la luz de tu hermosura,
alevemente violenta,
mirando lo que me halague,
no veré lo que me ofenda.
Pensarás que, como suele
en la enemiga ribera
el cocodrilo atraer
al peregrino a sus quejas,
y, alevosa la piedad,
a su rüina le lleva,
que así tú, al hechizo blando
de tus fingidas cautelas,
aunque el peligro conozca,
harás que al peligro vuelva.
Mas con una distinción,
que el cocodrilo lamenta
y llora al que ya mató;
mas tú, si mi muerte vieras,
hicieras risa a mi muerte
aun más fiera que las fieras.

Y así, no pienses, ingrata,
que vengo a darte las quejas
de mis pasados agravios,
porque ya de tus ofensas
estoy tan desengañado
que las prisiones violentas,
que me echaron tus traiciones,
no sólo al alma molestan,
mas, rotos los eslabones,
el desengaño no deja
ni aun la más leve memoria
del ruido de las cadenas.
Pensarás . . .

DOÑA ANA Don Juan, no pases
adelante, porque es fuerza
que, cuando ofendes mi amor,
también mi decoro ofendas.

TACON Y demás de eso, también
es muy grande impertinencia
el que quiera adivinar
lo que piensas o no piensas.

DON JUAN Calla, Tacón, si no quieres
usar mal de mi paciencia.

TACON Señor, me ha dado una joya,
y he de estar en su defensa.

DOÑA ANA Vuelvo a decir que mi amor
y mi honor igual ofensa
injustamente padecen
en tus mal fundadas quejas.
Los celos, don Juan, los celos,
y el nombrarlos yo no sea
indecoro, porque, cuando
para explicarse las penas
está el estudio en las voces,
muy ociosa está la queja.
Los celos —vuelvo a decir—
no son más que una quimera[21]

---

[21] "Chimera" en 1681, pero se pronunciaba entonces como "quimera". Véase "chimera" en *Autoridades.*

que allá el pensamiento forma
por que* allá se desvanezca; para que
una sospecha villana
son: ¿es posible que creas
mucho más que a un amor noble,
a una villana sospecha?
Si tú la evidencia hallaras . . .

DON JUAN Pues di, ¿qué más evidencia
que el hallar hablando un hombre,
ingrata, a la misma reja
en que tú hablabas conmigo?

DOÑA ANA ¿No hay una criada que pueda
ser desleal?

DON JUAN Las crïadas
siempre son disculpas hechas
para cualquiera traición.

TACON Y más si es moza gallega.[22]

DON JUAN ¿Ya no te he dicho que calles?

DOÑA ANA Pues, don Juan, para que sepas
la verdad de todo el lance
y contigo no padezca
mi honor, ya que tu mudanza
desengañada me deja,
sabe, en fin, cómo don Diego
de Guevara, con promesas
y dádivas, granjeó
una criada por que* fuera para que
medianera de un amor
que en mi desprecio fue ofensa;
esta desleal traidora
fue la que habló por la reja
con él cuando tú llegaste.
Mira tú cómo pudiera
de doméstica malicia
eximirse mi inocencia.

DON JUAN ([*Aparte*] ¡Raro caso! A mi enemigo
fue a quien defendí.)

---

[22] Para la actitud de los españoles hacia las mozas gallegas, véase Herrero García, pp. 209–13.

DOÑA ANA ¿En qué piensas?
Ya yo he vuelto por mi honor,
y pues tú mismo confiesas
que ya se acabó tu amor
y se olvidó tu fineza,
vuélvete donde jamás,
ingrato, te oiga ni vea,
y no llame mi venganza
a la razón de mi ofensa;
véte, ingrato, desatento.

Sale DOÑA BEATRIZ.

DOÑA BEATRIZ Prima, ¿qué voces son ésas?
Mas tienes mucha razón;
éste el hombre es que en la selva
me siguió, y el que atrevido,
sin que mis desprecios sienta,
vino anoche a referirme
los afectos de su necia
pasión; y así tú, doña Ana,
hazle que cese en su tema.
Dile quién soy y quién eres,
por que* otra vez no se atreva para que
a arriesgar nuestro decoro,
sabiendo lo que se arriesga. *Vase.*
TACON Buenos han quedado; esto es
caerse la casa acuestas;
no es malo querer a dos,
mas tiene estas contingencias.
DOÑA ANA Pensaréis, señor don Juan,
que os he de dar muchas quejas,
a vista de aqueste agravio;
pensáis mal, que las ofensas
conocidas, las castiga
mejor la que las desprecia.
Pensaréis . . .
TACON Déjate ahora
de si piensa o si no piensa;
sino quítate un chapín
y rómpele la cabeza,

que tendrás mucha razón.
DON JUAN Pícaro, tu desvergüenza
ya no es sufrible.
DOÑA ANA Teneos,
no así el crïado os divierta;
decidme, ¿qué hemos de hacer
de aquellas tibias pavesas,
de la incauta mariposa,
de la enemiga ribera,
del cocodrilo?
DON JUAN No así,
ingrata, te ensoberbezca
una razón, que lo[23] es
solamente en la apariencia.
DOÑA ANA Según eso, ¿no seguiste
aquesta dama en las selvas?
DON JUAN Esa fue cortesanía.
DOÑA ANA ¿Y el venir anoche a verla?
¿Qué fue?[24]
DON JUAN A eso responder
te puedo con evidencia,
que vine sólo a buscar
al señor don Luis con estas
cartas, y tú te turbaste
al mirarme de manera
que confirmaste mi agravio.
DOÑA ANA Muy buena disculpa es ésa.
DON JUAN Mucho mejor que la tuya.
DOÑA ANA Yo en casa tengo quien sea
testigo de mi razón.
DON JUAN Pues yo tengo fuera della
un galán que habla de noche.
DOÑA ANA ¿Qué querías? ¿Que volviera
ahora a satisfacerte?[25]

---

[23] Dialefa entre "lo" y "es".

[24] Dialefa entre "fue" y "A".

[25] "Queríais que volviera / ahora a satisfaceros?" en BNM1, BNM2, BAE y TS. Creo que debe haber el tuteo aquí para dar luego realce al cambio de actitud de doña Ana.

Don Juan, ahorremos[26] de quejas:
vos estéis muy bien hallado
con otro amor, yo contenta
también con mi desengaño;
pues hagamos los dos cuenta
que esto se ha acabado.[27]

DON JUAN Aunque
sé tu intención, norabuena.

DOÑA ANA Norabuena; adiós.

DON JUAN Adiós.

TACON Aunque mil vidas perdiera,
no había de dejarte ir,
sin que quede satisfecha
aquesta pobre señora.

DON JUAN Pícaro, no me detengas.

DOÑA ANA Déjale, Tacón,

TACON No quiero,
que es muy grande desvergüenza
que no te pida perdón.

DON JUAN Suelta, borracho.

TACON ¿Qué es suelta?

Saca la daga DON JUAN, y DOÑA ANA le detiene, y TACON se va a entrar, y salen [DOÑA] BEATRIZ, CELESTINA, INES y ANTONIA, y le detienen.

DON JUAN Vive Dios, que no dejara
de romperte la cabeza,
infame.

DOÑA ANA Don Juan, ¿qué es esto?
¿Qué desatención es ésta?

TACON Tenle, que es un diablo cuando
se envibora y se enserpienta.[28]

DOÑA BEATRIZ Hombre, ¿dónde vas?

ANTONIA Detente.

---

[26] Sinéresis en "ahorremos".

[27] Dialefa entre "acabado" y "Aunque".

[28] Véase *Elegir al enemigo*, de Salazar, vv. 1992–1999.

CELESTINA Aguarda.
TACON No me detengan.
DON JUAN Vive Dios . . .
DOÑA ANA No has de pasar
adelante.
DON JUAN La insolencia
de ese pícaro . . .

Sale DON LUIS.

DON LUIS ¿Qué es esto?
¿Cómo? ¿En mi casa pendencias?
DOÑA ANA ¡Ay de mí!
DON JUAN ¡Válgame el cielo!
DOÑA BEATRIZ ¡Qué miro!
DON LUIS ¿Tú tan suspensa,
doña Ana? ¿Tú tan turbada,
Beatriz?[29] ¿Qué es esto?
CELESTINA En conciencia,
que no es nada, sino que
hay mujeres hazañeras.
DON LUIS Pues decid vos lo que ha sido.
TACON Dios ponga tiento en tu lengua*. prudencia
CELESTINA ¿Ya te acuerdas de la joya
que dio esta mañana mesma
su tío a doña Ana?
DON LUIS Muy bien.
CELESTINA Pues para ponerla nueva
cinta, que al tocado diga,
la puso sobre esa mesa,
y, entrando a sacar las cintas,
hallando franca la puerta,
subió el ladrón que allí miras.
TACON ¿Cómo que?
CELESTINA Pero al cogerla,
quiso la buena fortuna
que salió Antonia. El, al verla,
partió a correr con la joya;

[29] Sinéresis en "Beatriz".

ella se fue por la reja . . .
TACON ¡Vive Dios!
CELESTINA . . . diciendo a voces:
"Señores, a ese hombre tengan,
que lleva hurtada una joya."
A este tiempo por la puerta
pasaba este caballero;
y, viendo tal desvergüenza,
sacó la daga; él de miedo
volvió a subir la escalera.
Mas tu hija, de pïadosa,
que no le siga le ruega,
temiendo que le matase.
Yo hice que le detuvieran
las demás.
TACON ¡Que esto me pase!
CELESTINA Y todo esto se remedia
con que le quiten la joya
y le den a buena cuenta
tanta cantidad de palos
que no[30] huelgue la madera.
DOÑA BEATRIZ ([*Aparte*] Esforcemos su mentira.)
DON LUIS ¡Ay tan grande desvergüenza!
Venid acá, ladronazo.
DOÑA ANA ([*Aparte*] Disimula.
DON JUAN ¿Que me adviertas
eso, sabiendo quién soy?)
DON LUIS ¿Qué es de la joya?
ANTONIA Al cogerla,
vi que la metió en el pecho.

Sácanle del pecho la joya.

CELESTINA Vesla aquí.
TACON ¡Que me suceda
esto por una borracha!
DON LUIS ¡Ay semejante insolencia!
¿Que aun repliquéis, ladronazo?

---

[30] Dialefa entre "no" y "huelgue".

Idos, pero no os suceda
que yo os vuelva a ver, y ahora
agradeced que no os llevan
adonde en una horca paguéis[31]
vuestro delito.

DOÑA ANA ¿Qué esperas,
hombre? Véte, pues que ves
de mi padre la clemencia.

TACON Sin honra y sin joya voy
por una infame hechicera.
¡Venganza, cielos, venganza!
¡Paciencia, cielos, paciencia! *Vase.*

DON LUIS Vos, caballero, viváis
mil años por tan atenta
acción.

DON JUAN En mí fue el serviros
dicha de la contingencia,
porque a traeros[32] estas cartas
venía[33] cuando la insolencia
sucedió de este ladrón.

DON LUIS De mi sobrino es la letra;
mucho tengo que estimaros.

DON JUAN El señor don Pedro queda
muy bueno y muy gran soldado.

DON LUIS Vos le honráis; mas por que* pueda — para que
yo buscaros y serviros,
saber el nombre merezca.

DON JUAN Mi nombre es don Juan de Lara.
Si queréis que la respuesta
vaya por mi mano a Flandes,
yo mismo vendré por ella.

DON LUIS Eso no, yo os buscaré.

DON JUAN Pues ahora,[34] dadme licencia,
porque, como llegué anoche,
tengo algunas dependencias

---

[31] El verso sería eneasílabo, a no ser pronunciada "paguéis" "págueis".

[32] Sinéresis en "traeros".

[33] Sinéresis en "venía".

[34] Sinéresis en "ahora".

precisas a que acudir.
DON LUIS — Mirad si yo puedo en ellas
serviros.
DON JUAN — Viváis mil años.
DON LUIS — Venid.
DOÑA ANA — ([*Aparte*]Decirte quisiera . . .
DON JUAN — Ya, ingrata, sé lo que quieres
decirme: que acá no vuelva.
DOÑA ANA — No es eso.
DON JUAN — Pues . . .).[35]
DON LUIS — Por aquí,
señor don Juan, es la puerta.
DON JUAN — Quedad con Dios. *Vase.*
DON LUIS — El os guarde.
¿Veslo, hija, como fue cuerda
prevención el advertirte
que con la casa tuvieras
gran cuidado?
CELESTINA — Cada día
suceden cosas como éstas.
DON LUIS — ¿Quién es aquesta mujer?
¿Es alguna criada nueva?
DOÑA ANA — No, señor; vino a vender
aderezos de Bohemia
de los que ahora se[36] usan.
DON LUIS — Pues yo quiero haceros ferias
dellos a ti y a Beatriz.[37]
([*Aparte*] El disimular es fuerza
por desmentir mi cuidado.)
DOÑA ANA — Mucho estimo tu fineza.
DOÑA BEATRIZ — Cuando las dos no tenemos
otro galán, ¿no era fuerza
que nos festeje mi tío?
DON LUIS — Ea, déles por mi cuenta
todo lo que la pidieren.
CELESTINA — Lo haré muy enhorabuena.

---

[35] Pongo el aparte aquí para aclarar la acción entre don Juan y doña Ana.
[36] Dialefa entre "se" y "usan".
[37] Sinéresis en "Beatriz".

DON LUIS ¿Cómo os llamáis?
CELESTINA Celestina.
DON LUIS ([*Aparte*] ¡Celestina! Esta es aquella
insigne mujer de quien
en toda Sevilla cuentan
raras cosas, aun los hombres
de más juicio, más prudencia
y más doctos.) Celestina,
déles todo cuanto quieran
escoger; y por que* no para que
embarace mi presencia,
ahora quedad con Dios,
porque ciertas diligencias
tengo que me dan cuidado.
([*Aparte*] De aquesta mujer la ciencia
en magía[38] y astrología,
dicen que no habrá quién pueda
imitarla; no sé qué
el corazón me aconseja
para salir del cuidado
que me aflige y atormenta.)
Adiós, hija; adiós, Beatriz.[39] *Vase.*
CELESTINA Digo, ¿quedábades buenas,[40]
si no fuera por mi industria?
DOÑA BEATRIZ Tú forjaste de manera
el cuento que no quedó
aun la más leve sospecha
de ser verdad.
CELESTINA Mi doña Ana,
¿de qué es aquesa tristeza?
DOÑA BEATRIZ Mira si te dije yo,
prima, que el hombre pudiera
ponernos en un empeño.
DOÑA ANA ¡Ay, Beatriz!,[41] deja que sienta
que, sin tener tú la culpa,

---

[38] Se prouncíaba como trísilabo.
[39] Sinéresis en "Beatriz".
[40] Véase la nota del v. 1445.
[41] Sinéresis en "Beatriz".

seas causa de mis penas.
DOÑA BEATRIZ ¿Yo causa de tus pesares?
DOÑA ANA No estoy para darte cuenta
ahora de mis desdichas;
antes me darás licencia
para que yo allá conmigo
me acompañe con mis quejas. *Vase.*
ANTONIA Voy a seguir a mi[42] ama. *[Vase.]*
DOÑA BEATRIZ Celestina, di, ¿qué lleva
mi prima?
CELESTINA Lleva unos celos,
que es un dolor de cabeza
que consiste en aprehensión,
pues duran lo que se piensan.
DOÑA BEATRIZ Y ¿quién se los causa?
CELESTINA Tú.
DOÑA BEATRIZ ¿Yo?
CELESTINA Sí, porque el que en la selva
te habló, y el que vino anoche,
es su amante.
DOÑA BEATRIZ ¿Qué ése[43] era
don Juan de Lara?
CELESTINA ¿Eso ignoras?
DOÑA BEATRIZ No puedo satisfacerla
más que con aborrecerle.
¡Qué poco don Diego hiciera
semejantes falsedades!
CELESTINA De ningún amante creas
que no esté expuesto a mudanzas,
porque el amor en cualquiera
hace sus torres de viento[44]
y les pone sus veletas.
DOÑA BEATRIZ Yo quiero creer lo contrario;
y puesto que tu fineza
se determina a buscarle,

---

[42] Dialefa entre "mi" y "ama".

[43] Dialefa entre "ese" y "era".

[44] *Torre de viento*—"Metaphoricamente se llama el pensamiento, ò discurso, con que alguna persona vanamente se persuade à sus conveniencias, y utilidades, ò à ostentar grandezas" (*Autoridades*).

te suplico que esto sea
luego, porque los cuidados
aguardan con impaciencia.

CELESTINA Digo que tienes razón,
adiós, queda satisfecha
de que yo le buscaré.

DOÑA BEATRIZ Pues mira que, hasta que venga,
quedo esperando y temiendo.

CELESTINA ¡Oh quién llevarte pudiera
a palacio, que es adonde
ni se teme ni se espera! *Vase.*

DOÑA BEATRIZ A pesar de la esperanza, [*romances*]
mal se alienta una pasión
cuando es dudoso el remedio
y es evidente el dolor.

INES Cree que, en teniendo noticia
don Diego de tu aflicción,
que él busque el remedio.

Al paño[45] *DON DIEGO.*

DON DIEGO Ya
que me ofrece esta ocasión
la fortuna, pues don Luis
vi que de casa salió,
hablar a doña Ana intento;
sepa que adorando estoy
aun sus desdenes; allí
está; ánimo, corazón,
que no ha de ser el afecto
hijo siempre del temor.

INES Si don Diego de Guevara
desde Granada pasó
con evidencia a Sevilla,
¿qué recelas?

DOÑA BEATRIZ El que no

---

[45] *Al paño* —"Phrase usada en los theatros de Comedias, que se dice del que está à la cortina que cubre el vestuario, como en escucha, y por extension se dice en otras ocasiónes" (*Aut* .).

es fácil que quien le busca
sepa dónde está.

Sale DON DIEGO.

DON DIEGO Aquí estoy,
hermosísima doña Ana . . .
mas . . . ¡Qué miro! ¿Es ilusión?
¿Aquí Beatriz?[46]
DOÑA BEATRIZ ¿De qué[47] es,
don Diego, la confusión?
DON DIEGO Yo, Beatriz,[48] si . . . cuando . . . como . . .
DOÑA BEATRIZ Si mi prima te llamó
en nombre mío, ¿de qué
procede tu turbación?
DON DIEGO ([*Aparte*] Ya aquí es preciso fingir.)
Beatriz,[49] de mi admiración
puedes argüir mi fineza;
pues como aquel que cegó,
si vuelve a cobrar la vista,
le deslumbra el esplendor;
así, al volver a mirar,
después de la intermisión
de nuestra ausencia, en tus ojos
el dulce divino ardor
me deslumbran dos luceros,
si me alumbra todo un sol.
DOÑA BEATRIZ Deja las cortesanías,
que imaginaré que no
son verdades tus finezas,
si exageraciones son.
DON DIEGO Poco de mi amor confías.
DOÑA BEATRIZ Tanto fío de tu amor
que tú el alivio has de ser
de una pena, de un dolor

---

[46] Sinéresis de "Beatriz".
[47] Dialefa entre "que" y "es".
[48] Sinéresis de "Beatriz".
[49] Sinéresis de "Beatriz".

que cabe en el sentimiento,
pero no en la explicación,
que para eso te he llamado.
DON DIEGO Si he de remediarlo yo,
presto saldrás del cuidado
que te aflige.[50]
DOÑA BEATRIZ Y así yo
lo creo de tu fineza;
mas por que* el pesar que[51] hoy para que
me aflige mejor lo sepas
de quien lo dirá mejor,
que siempre se explica más
quien tiene menos pasión . . .
¡Inés!
INES ¿Señora?
DOÑA BEATRIZ A mi prima
llama.
INES A obedecerte voy. *Vase.*
DON DIEGO ¿Para qué ha sido el llamarla?
DOÑA BEATRIZ Porque era desatención,
habiéndola dado cuenta
de mi cuidado y tu amor,
no conferirlo con ella;
y era especie de traición
el ocultarte en su casa.

Sale DOÑA ANA.

DOÑA ANA A pesar de mi dolor,
vengo a ver lo que me mandas.
¡Qué miro!
DON DIEGO Perdido soy.
DOÑA ANA Pues ¿cómo vos, atrevido,
intentáis . . . ?
DOÑA BEATRIZ Tu indignación
prima, mira que es injusta,
que éste es don Diego, a quien yo

[50] Dialefa entre "aflige" e "Y".
[51] Dialefa entre "que" y "hoy".

debí la vida en Granada,
y a quien llamamos las dos
para que el alivio sea
de mi cuidado.

DOÑA ANA Pues no
es justo que yo te engañe:
éste es, Beatriz,[52] el que dio
principio a todos mis males;
éste es el que hizo traidor
desleales mis crïadas;
déste la vana pasión
hoy ocasiona mis penas;
no me permitas que yo,
pues mi dolor lloro, calle
la causa de mi dolor.

DOÑA BEATRIZ No era, no, tirano aleve,
en vano tu turbación.

DOÑA ANA ¿Cuándo no temió un delito?

DOÑA BEATRIZ Y no has de quedar, traidor,
sin castigo.

DOÑA ANA No le[53] hay
a tanta ofensa.

DON DIEGO Si no
me oís las dos, quedaré
bien a un tiempo con las dos,
porque disculpa el delito
no oír la satisfacción.

LAS DOS Pues ¿cuál puede ser?

DON DIEGO Aquésta:
en ti, doña Ana, mi amor
fue desdichado y primero;
luego me dio la ocasión
la hermosura de Beatriz,[54]
y la fortuna el favor
para segundo cuidado.
Decidme: ¿el que idolatró

---

[52] Sinéresis en "Beatriz".
[53] Dialefa entre "le" y "hay".
[54] Sinéresis en "Beatriz".

las estrellas, por que* vea — para que
de la que se anticipó
el esplendor, a las otras
les negará el esplendor?
¿El que en el culto jardín
vio la rosa y celebró
la púrpura, del jazmín
después no alabó el candor?
¿El que del dulce silguero* — jilguero
oyó la sonora voz,
dejará de celebrar
lo tierno del ruiseñor?
En el nácar, si dos perlas
tienen igual perfección,
¿le quitará la primera
a la segunda el valor?
Pues, yo así, aunque de tus ojos,
doña Ana, sentí el ardor,
mirándome despechado,
di el culto a otra perfección
a la tuya igual; y así,
nunca he ofendido a las dos,
pues adoré vuestras luces
iguales, como el que vio
sucesivos el lucero,
la perla, el ave y la flor.[55]

DOÑA ANA Buena disculpa es aquésa
para ser contra mi honor
escándalo de mi casa.

DOÑA BEATRIZ Bueno es que quieras, traidor,
por disculpa introducir
fineza en amar a dos.
Y así, ingrato . . .[56]

DOÑA ANA Y así, aleve . . .

DOÑA BEATRIZ . . . si tu engaño . . .

DOÑA ANA . . . tu traición . . .

DOÑA BEATRIZ . . . intentare . . .

---

[55] Vv. 2020–46 son ejemplo de diseminación-recolección.

[56] Dialefa entre "ingrato" e "Y".

DOÑA ANA . . . presumiere . . .
DON DIEGO Si me atendéis . . .

Sale INES.

INES Mi señor
está ya en la calle.
DOÑA ANA ¡Cielos,
esto faltaba!
DON DIEGO ¡Quién vio
tanto tropel de cuidados!
INES No[57] hay más remedio, sino
el que don Diego se esconda.
DOÑA BEATRIZ Pues, ¿qué aguardáis?
DON DIEGO Vuestro honor
sólo ocultarme podía.
INES Venid.
DON DIEGO Ya te sigo. *[Vanse.]*
DOÑA ANA No
nos encuentre aquí mi padre;
retirémonos las dos
a mi cuarto.
DOÑA BEATRIZ Vamos, pues.
¡Ah ciego, ah tirano amor!
¡Qué de cuidados me cuestas!
DOÑA ANA ¿Cuándo no fue propensión
suya el que sea[58] mensajero
un dolor de otro dolor? *Va[n]se.*

---

[57] Dialefa entre "No" y "hay".

[58] Sinéresis en "sea".

CUADRO II[59]

Sale[n] DON LUIS y CELESTINA.

CELESTINA Decidme, señor don Luis,
¿qué mandáis?
DON LUIS Gran confusión
te causará, Celestina,
el que te aguardase yo
para traerte conmigo.
CELESTINA Lo que sé sólo es que estoy
pronta a cuánto me mandares.
DON LUIS ([*Aparte*] ¡Cuánto puede una pasión!
¡A cuánto obliga un cuidado!
¡Y más si es como el que yo
padezco!)
CELESTINA ([*Aparte*] ¿Qué es lo que intenta
este viejo?)
DON LUIS ([*Aparte*] Si el dolor
que me aflige[60] y atormenta,
víbora del corazón,
ha de quitarme la vida
y con la vida el honor,
nadie se admire que tome
tan ardua resolución
como la que ahora emprendo;
y más cuando cierto estoy
que della ha de proceder
mi quietud.)
CELESTINA Dime, señor,
¿a qué me has traído?
DON LUIS Sabe,

[59] El dramaturgo ha creado un cuadro nuevo para preparar la escena del espejo. Sugiero que, en una producción en un corral, el espejo se montaba en lo que J. E. Varey ha llamado en muchos estudios "la escena interior," o "the discovery space" en el teatro isabelino. En la corte, habría un montaje similar, en el centro del tablado. En el grabado de TS, el artista nos da un espejo enorme, indicando su importancia en la acción de la comedia.

[60] Dialefa entre "aflige" e "y".

lo que he de fiarte[61] hoy
es no menos que un secreto
en que consiste mi honor.

CELESTINA Yo estimo la confianza.

DON LUIS Yo sé con la perfección
que magia y astrología[62]
sabes, y con el primor
que ejecutas sus prodigios;
tú me has de decir . . .

CELESTINA Señor,
advierte . . .

DON LUIS No hay que excusarte,
que no te buscara yo
a no ser así; y en fe
de aquesta satisfacción,
sabe que me has de decir
quién es un hombre que habló
anoche por una reja
de mi jardín.

CELESTINA ¿Cómo yo,
señor, puedo adivinarlo?

DON LUIS Yo sé hasta dónde llegó
tu ciencia; y advierte que
te he revelado mi honor;
y si en lo que te pregunto
no veo la ejecución,
he de quitarte la vida,
porque yo mi pundonor
no he de fiar de tu secreto.
Pero si me hicieres hoy
este gusto, pues que puedes,
tú tendrás tal galardón
que no quepa en tu deseo;
y entonces quedaré yo
satisfecho del secreto,
pues también importa, y no
te ha de valer el ardid

[61] Dialefa entre "fiarte" y "hoy".
[62] Véase v. 1851.

de algún engaño o ficción;
porque el que dijeres que es
el que en mi jardín habló,
he de ir luego a examinarlo.

CELESTINA ¿Quién se vio en tal aflicción?

DON LUIS Y has de quedar encerrada
hasta saber si es, o no,
verdad lo que me dijeres.
Toma la resolución
de lo que debes hacer.

CELESTINA ([*Aparte*] Aquí Celestina dio
fin a todos sus enredos.)
Mira . . .

DON LUIS No te he de oír razón.

CELESTINA Advierte . . .

CELESTINA No hay que advertir.
Escoger una de dos:
o morir o lo que he dicho
ponerlo en ejecución.

CELESTINA ¿Ni querrás darme siquiera
término para que yo
pueda hacer mis diligencias?

DON LUIS Eso está puesto en razón*; razonable
piensa, pues, lo que has de hacer,
en tanto que a escribir voy
una carta en este cuarto,
y luego volveré. Adiós. *Vase.*

CELESTINA "¿O morir o lo que he dicho
ponerlo en ejecución?"
¿Estamos buenos? Ya aquí
Celestina feneció;
su buena opinión la mata,
porque la buena opinión
siempre fue contra su dueño.
Pero ahora es lo peor
que no me puedo valer
de engaño ni de invención,
por ingeniosa que sea,
que este viejo faraón,
después de echar la sentencia,
a la sentencia añadió:

"Y has de quedar encerrada
hasta saber si es, o no,
verdad lo que me dijeres;"
con que es preciso que[63] hoy
no sólo pierda la vida,
pero la reputación
que me han dado mis enredos,
que tanto afán y sudor
me han costado. ¡Ah desdichada!
¿Cómo en la ocasión mejor,
embustes, me habéis dejado?
Mas ¿cuándo no sucedió
que los conocidos falten
en la mejor ocasión?
Moriré en fin.

Salen DOÑA ANA y DOÑA BEATRIZ.

DOÑA ANA Celestina.
CELESTINA ¿Qué queréis?
DOÑA ANA Inés nos dio
noticia de como estabas
aquí.
DOÑA BEATRIZ Tú de una aflicción
nos has de sacar.
CELESTINA Aquesto
le faltaba a mi dolor.
DOÑA ANA Sabe que un hombre escondido
tenemos.
DOÑA BEATRIZ Vida y honor,
si le encontrara mi tío,
perdemos[64] doña Ana y yo.
DOÑA ANA En aqueste cuarto está
oculto; mira que no
nos dejes en tanto empeño,
pues puedes hacerlo. Adiós.
DOÑA BEATRIZ Adiós, y mira que vamos

[63] Dialefa entre "que" y "hoy".
[64] "Perdiéramos" o, como es ordinario en Salazar, "perdíamos".

confiadas en ti. *Vanse.*

CELESTINA ¿Quién vio
tanto tropel de aflicciones?
Mas siempre los males son
como los vasos de noria,
que el uno al otro siguió;
y quien los padece es como
quien los anda alrededor.[65]
Mas ¿qué es esto? ¿Yo me aflijo?
¿O soy Celestina o no?
¿Yo no sé que he de morir?
Pues ánimo, corazón,
que, de lo peor[66] que suceda,
el morir es lo peor.
¡Ah caballero escondido!

Sale DON DIEGO.

DON DIEGO ¿Quién me ha llamado?

CELESTINA Yo soy

DON DIEGO ¿Es Celestina?

CELESTINA ¿Don Diego?

DON DIEGO ¿Qué intentas?

CELESTINA Que, cuando yo
te llamare, al punto salgas.

DON DIEGO A cualquiera trance estoy
expuesto.

CELESTINA Pues ten cuidado
en llegando la ocasión,
y ahora vuelve a esconderte.

DON DIEGO ¡Rara mujer! *Escóndese.*

CELESTINA Desde[67] hoy
mejorada en tercio y quinto
ha de quedar mi opinión;
porque ... pero ello dirá.

---

[65] O sea, es un asno.
[66] Sinéresis en "peor".
[67] Dialefa entre "desde" y "hoy".

Sale DON LUIS.

DON LUIS ¿Celestina?
CELESTINA Ya, señor,
me resolví a obedecerte;
y es cierto que tu aflicción,
mucho más que tu amenaza,
a servirte mi obligó.
DON LUIS No lo perderás de mí.
CELESTINA Ven acá; ¿tendrás valor?
DON LUIS Yo nunca conozco al miedo.
CELESTINA Pues por que* veas que no (para que)
puedes padecer engaño,
el que en tu jardín habló
he de enseñarte visible.
DON LUIS ¿Adónde?
CELESTINA En la reflexión
de ese espejo.[68]
DON LUIS ¡Quién pensara
nunca que a tanto llegó
la ciencia de una mujer!
CELESTINA Desde aquí pon atención
al reflejo del cristal,
sin que con vista o acción
te diviertas a otra parte
hasta que te avise yo,
que él se mostrará visible
al conjuro de mi voz.
DON LUIS Ya te obedezco, aunque ponen
aquestos casos horror.
CELESTINA Pues ea, manos a la obra.
Oh tú, en cualquiera región
que te hallares, aunque sea
la que no calienta el sol
o dora la blanca luna,
aunque el abismo mayor
te oculte en su obscuro caos,

[68] La acción de los vv. 2236 y siguientes trae a la memoria un truco similar en *La cueva de Salamanca* de Cervantes.

al precepto de mi voz
ven al instante, y pasando
visible en la reflexión
deste espejo . . .

Va pasando DON DIEGO.

DON DIEGO Ya es preciso
el salir.
CELESTINA . . . a la atención
de quien desea[69] conocerte
te muestra.
DON LUIS ¡Qué confusión!
Ya le veo, ya le veo.
CELESTINA No te muevas.
DON LUIS Ya pasó.
CELESTINA ¿Ha pasado?
DON LUIS Ya ha pasado.
CELESTINA En fin, don Luis mi señor,
esto se ha hecho sin desgracia.
DON LUIS ¡Qué pasmo! ¡Qué admiración!

Sale DOÑA BEATRIZ.

DOÑA BEATRIZ ¿Qué es esto?

Sale DOÑA ANA.

DOÑA ANA ¿De qué das voces?
DON LUIS No podré daros razón
del dolor que me atormenta,
si me la quita el dolor . . .
¿Celestina?
CELESTINA ¿Qué me mandas?
¿Hasle conocido?
DON LUIS No,
y eso es lo que más me aflige;

[69] Sinéresis en "desea".

mañana te veré yo,
pues ahora no podemos
discurrir. Adiós.
CELESTINA Adiós.
DON LUIS ([*Aparte*] Mas si el que vi en el espejo
fuese . . . pero es ilusión.) *Vase.*
DOÑA BEATRIZ ¿Qué es aquesto, Celestina?
CELESTINA Que don Diego se escapó,
y que habéis quedado libres.
DOÑA ANA Mal consuela a un corazón
quitarle un pesar, si queda
en el pecho otro mayor.
CELESTINA Esa no es muy buena cuenta,
porque uno y uno son dos.
DOÑA BEATRIZ Tú, Celestina, el remedio,
pues unas las penas son,
has de ser de nuestras penas.
DOÑA ANA Por que* no venza una error. para que
DOÑA BEATRIZ Por que* no triunfe un engaño. para que
CELESTINA Y porque tenéis razón,
y porque ya lo conozco,
y porque sí y porque no.

JORNADA TERCERA

CUADRO I

Sale[n] DON LUIS y CELESTINA

CELESTINA ¡Mucho habéis madrugado, [*silvas de consonantes*]
señor don Luis!
DON LUIS Cuando es grande un cuidado,
¿que es, Celestina, ignoras
despertador sin término en las horas?
CELESTINA Son, al quitar el sueño, los pesares
pulgas, con quien no valen los pulgares,
pues cuando el pecho asaltan,
por más que hayan picado, nunca faltan;
en fin, ¿qué es lo que mandas?
DON LUIS Lo que quiero
es saber hoy de ti, pero primero
toma esta joya, y sólo en ella intento
principio dar a mi agradecimiento.
CELESTINA Aqueso era excusado, en mi conciencia.
DON LUIS Más debo yo a tu ciencia;
en fin, lo que pretende
mi dolor, pues he visto al que me ofende
de aquel mágico espejo
en el mudo reflejo,
es ahora tener dél noticia cierta,
y inquirir . . . Mas llamaron a la puerta. *Llaman.*
CELESTINA Veré quién es.
DON LUIS Que no me vea intento.
CELESTINA Pues en ese aposento
te puedes ocultar, que yo al instante
intento despachar este marchante.
DON LUIS Pues no te tardes.
CELESTINA Cierra bien la puerta;

Escóndese DON LUIS.

y el auditorio advierta
que esta comedia ha sido
la primera en que el viejo se ha escondido.
¿Quién es? ¿Tacon?

TACON — Aquí vengo [*romances*]
de mi desdicha forzado.

CELESTINA — Mejor fuera de galera.

TACON — Mejor te lleven los diablos.

CELESTINA — Mas que ya has rompido* el nombre, roto
y que, a fuer de buen soldado,
de potable polverín
has cargado con los frascos.[1]

TACON — Pues ven acá, mosquetera
de tiros tan acertados,
que, aunque le apuntes al tinto,
también le aciertas al blanco,
¿a mí te vienes con eso?

CELESTINA — ¿No haremos paces un rato,
Tacon?

TACON — ¿Yo contigo paces?
¿Cuándo ayer, a un hombre honrado,
no solamente quitaste
la[2] honra, que no es del caso,
sino una joya?

CELESTINA — Ya viste
que fue imposible excusarlo.

TACON — Pues ¿no podías hacernos
invisibles a mi[3] amo
y a mí?

---

[1] Al mencionar la palabra "diablos," Tacón debe asumir la responsabilidad del peligro que pueda suceder. Mencionar el nombre del diablo en casa de Celestina es como llevar los frascos del polvorín. *Frasco*—"Se llama tambien el vaso hecho regularmente de madéra de áire, en que se lleva la pólvora para cargar la escopéta. Dixose asi por la figúra que tiene de frasco" (*Aut.*).

[2] Dialefa entre "la" y "honra".

[3] Dialefa entre "mi" y "amo".

CELESTINA No me fue posible,
porque en casa había[4] dejado
el conjuro de invisibles.
TACON Pues sabe que no has logrado
tu depravada intención,
porque si allí me quitaron
la joya, al punto doña Ana
este bolsillo me ha enviado
con cien escudos.
CELESTINA Por cierto,
que los goces muchos años,
¿que con eso no tendrás
invidia de que me han dado
a mí la joya?
TACON ¿La joya?
CELESTINA Vesla aquí.
TACON Fuera gran cargo
de mi conciencia, por cierto,
no cobrarme de mi mano
mi hacienda; de bueno a bueno
dame mi joya.
CELESTINA Borracho,
mira lo que intentas.
TACON Bruja,
embustera, bien mirado
lo tengo; y me la has de dar,
o he de romperte los cascos,
derramando más vendimias
que se hacen por Todos Santos.[5]
CELESTINA Mira que no me conoces.
TACON Pues ahora solos estamos,
yo no temo hechicerías.
¿Piensas hallarte a la mano
otro viejo que me tenga
por ladrón?
CELESTINA Si yo me enfado,

[4] Sinéresis en "había".

[5] El primero de noviembre, fiesta de Todos los Santos, también es el tiempo de recolección y cosecha de la uva

el mismo que allá te tuvo
por ladrón vendrá volando,
y hará ponerte en la[6] horca.

TACON Eso veremos, en tanto
que yo te quito mi joya.

CELESTINA Suelta, pícaro, bellaco,
bufón.

Quiere quitarle la joya.

TACON Deja, encorozada.[7]

CELESTINA Señor don Luis, vuestro amparo
me valga; de dondequiera
que estéis, salid, que un malvado
ladrón intenta robarme.

Sale DON LUIS.

DON LUIS ¿Qué es aquesto, ladronazo?

TACON ¡Válgame San Babilés![8]
¡Vive Dios, que estoy temblando!

CELESTINA Señor, ya le conocéis,
este pícaro tacaño,
como le descubrí el hurto
en tu casa, él, esperando
ocasión para vengarse,
vino y, al punto mirando
la joya que tú me diste,
después de haberme llevado
un bolso con cien escudos
que tenía para el gasto
de casa sobre esa mesa,
me quiso quitar, porfiando
en que la joya era suya.

DON LUIS Por cierto muy bien ganado

---

6 Dialefa entre "la" y "horca".

7 *Encorozado*—de la coroza o capa de afrenta que se pone a los reos.

8 *San Babilés*—"Obispo y mártir, que se supone nacido en Pamplona, durante la Reconquista" (*En. E-C.*).

caudal para hacerlo vuestro.
Ahora[9] quiero yo entregaros . . .

TACON Señor.

DON LUIS . . . a quien luego al punto
os ponga, infame, en un palo,
y paguéis vuestros delitos,
porque, aunque yo castigaros
pudiera, mejor será
que deis ejemplo a los malos.
Venid, infame, ladrón.

TACON Señor fantasma . . . ([*Aparte*] Temblando
estoy del viejo estantigua*.) fantasma

CELESTINA Mucho mejor es dejarlo,
como me vuelva el bolsillo,
por no hacer ruido.

DON LUIS Volando,
dad luego esos cien escudos.

TACON Venlos aquí. ¡Cielos santos!,
¿a quién habrá sucedido,
por tan extraños acasos,
lo que a mí con esta infame
borracha?

CELESTINA Ea, ahora dejadlo,
señor don Luis.

DON LUIS Advirtiendo
que si en otra parte os hallo,
sin que valga intercesión,
al instante he da entregaros
donde os hagan cuartos.

TACON Eso
me será bien excusado,
porque yo voy a ahorcarme;
y pues soy tan desdichado,
que me quitan los doblones,
¿para qué quiero los cuartos?
Paciencia, cielos, paciencia.

DON LUIS ¿Aun replicáis, ladronazo?

CELESTINA Avísame si te ahorcares,

---

[9] Sinéresis en "ahora".

que yo pagaré el esparto★. dogal o cuerda
TACON No pagarás, que yo antes
haré que tengan el pago
que merecen tus embustes,
y así quedaré vengado. *Vase.*
DON LUIS Volvamos, pues, Celestina,
a repetir el cuidado
que más me aflige; éste[10] es
saber si el que de mi agravio
es dueño es acaso noble.
CELESTINA ([*Aparte*] Pues ya tengo averiguado
cuanto deseas saber,
porque Antonia me ha contado
que don Diego aquella noche
estuvo con ella hablando
por la reja del jardín.)
Caballero es estirado[11]
de lo mejor de Granada.
DON LUIS ¿Cómo se llama?
CELESTINA ([*Aparte*] Esto es malo,
porque puede contra mí
resultar algún porrazo,
si hay pendencia y se descubre
mi chisme, y también si callo
que es don Diego, y otro digo,
el viejo irá a averiguarlo,
y corro mayor peligro.)
DON LUIS Acaba, ¿qué estás dudando?
CELESTINA Yo señor . . .
DON LUIS ¿Qué es lo que temes?
CELESTINA No quisiera . . .
DON LUIS Dilo claro.
CELESTINA Si digo el nombre, tener
algún ruido o embarazo
que me saliese a la cara,
con que, al cabo de mis años,

[10] Dialefa entre "éste" y "es".

[11] *Estirado*—"Metaphoricamente vale grave, autorizado, principal, noble y digno de estimacion y aprecio" (*Aut.*).

venga a perder esta negra
honra que tanto he guardado.

DON LUIS
No tienes que recelar
nada, que en mí asegurado
te prometo que estará
el secreto, pues a entrambos
importa.

CELESTINA
Pues en fe deso,
te digo que el embozado
es don Diego de Guevara.

DON LUIS
¿Don Diego es? Bien mi cuidado,
al mirarle en el espejo,
lo sospechó; pero el pasmo
no me dejó conocerle,[12]
y ahora más indignado
debo estar de su traición;
pues conociéndonos tanto
don Diego y yo, y siendo[13] él
caballero, por tan bajos,
viles medios, el honor
quiere arriesgar de un anciano
padre y de una noble dama,
cuando con proporcionados
medios conseguir pudiera
con gusto mío la mano
de mi[14] hija; mas pues ya
le conozco, he de buscarlo,
y vive Dios que ha de ver . . .

CELESTINA
No te irrites.

DON LUIS
Tú me has dado
las noticias que deseaba;[15]
quédate adiós, que este caso
no pide más dilación.
Adiós.

---

[12] Véanse vv. 2279–80.

[13] Dialefa entre "siendo" y "él".

[14] Dialefa entre "mi" e "hija".

[15] Sinéresis en "deseaba".

Vase DON LUIS.

CELESTINA Adiós. Voy volando
a avisar a mis dos damas
de todo lo que ha pasado,
que quizá puede importar,
y a fe que el lance es bien arduo,
por el paso en que me veo,
con ser de comedia el paso. *Vase.*

En este estado dejó don Agustín la comedia, y desde aquí la prosigue quien saca sus obras a luz.

LA CONCLUSION DE VERA TASSIS

CUADRO II

Sale[n] DOÑA ANA y DOÑA BEATRIZ, y el espejo esté en la parte donde quedó antes.

DOÑA ANA De buen susto nos libramos. [*romances*]
DOÑA BEATRIZ La industria de Celestina
consiguió mañosamente
templar las crueles iras
de mi tío.[1]
DOÑA ANA Siempre un espejo
templó su crueldad impía,
que, como en él se retratan,
son de la razón mal vistas,
pues desfigura el reflejo
cuánto las pasiones pintan.
DOÑA BEATRIZ Y don Diego de Guevara
con buena sofistería
quiso probar ser fineza
querer a dos.
DOÑA ANA Fue precisa
la respuesta, que un amante,
si convencido se mira,
con el arte del ingenio
disculpa su grosería.
DOÑA BEATRIZ Grande lo fue el confesarnos
querer a dos.
DOÑA ANA Pues ya, prima,
puedes quedar consolada,
sabiendo que él de mis iras
sólo ha sido blanco inútil,

---

[1] Sinéresis en "tío".

que en su amor labró su ruina.
DOÑA BEATRIZ No tan rigurosa estés,
viendo que mi amor le estima,
pues aun no puede lo falso
borrarle del alma mía.
DOÑA ANA Prima, yo le aborreciera,
si, tan osado, a mi vista
a confesarme llegara
don Juan que a otra quería.
DOÑA BEATRIZ Bástame para consuelo
que no esté correspondida
su voluntad con la tuya,
y eso mi amistad te estima;
pero, al ver sus rendimientos,
justo es que mi amor te pida
que, pues no le correspondes,
no así le desprecies, prima;
que, cuando aquello agradezco,
esto el alma me fatiga.
Ya te he dicho que en Granada
libre del amor vivía,
burlando de sus arpones
la volante tiranía,
cuando en sus fragosos bosques,
en la caza divertida,
penetré lo más oculto,
buscando en la entretejida
selva la tímida fiera
que, sin que el plomo la rinda,
alterada con el ruido,
de su ardiente impulso huía.
Donde cazador astuto
don Diego el bosque seguía,
y me libró de las fieras
sangrientas crüeles iras
del bruto que me acosaba,
dejándome agradecida
lo noble de sus acciones,
que, cuando las atendía,
sentí acá en el corazón
una llama, aunque remisa,

y en el dominio del alma
una dulce tiranía,
que no pareció violencia;
una congoja bien quista
que, con los visos de agrado,
al pecho se introducía
por las puertas del oído
y ventanas de la vista.
Era un veneno letal
y una pena apetecida,
de tal suerte poderosa
que por no verla moría,
y también moría[2] por verla,
moríame por no oírla,
y por oírla también.
Con que en concorde milicia
batallaban mis pasiones
si le miraba o le oía,
y de mi razón triunfaban
estas blandas baterías,
quedando el alma gustosa
a sus esfuerzos rendida
si le oía o le miraba,
si no le escuchaba o vía*. veía
Permitíle que me viese,
y también le permitía
que me escribiera, después
que me hablara algunos días
en el campo y en mi casa,
para examinarle fina;
por estos correspondidos
dulces pasos discurría
al umbral de la esperanza,
que en las amantes fatigas
son los báculos[3] adonde
toda el alma se reclina.

---

[2] Sinéresis en "moría".

[3] *Báculo*—Dilogía que quiere decir alivio al mismo tiempo que palo en el cual apoyarse.

En esta, pues, dulce, aleve
suspensión mi amor vivía,
hasta que la suerte, ¡ah cielos!,
quiso llamarle a Sevilla
a unas graves dependencias
que con sus deudos tenía.
También mi padre a este tiempo
quiso que en Cádiz . . . —¡oh indigna
ley paternal, que pretendes
que un albedrío se rinda
a injusto tirano imperio,
sin que te venza o reprima
el ver que en dominio dulce
y en suave quietud tranquila
pone el cielo en libertad
lo mismo que tú cautivas!—
Quiso que en Cádiz casara
mi padre, otra vez repitan
mis labios, por ver si alguna
quiere despojar mi vida;
pero yo, firme y constante
en mi empeño . . .

Sale CELESTINA.

CELESTINA Señoritas,
¿cómo del pasado riesgo
os halláis?
DOÑA ANA Yo, Celestina,
con más engaños que sustos.
DOÑA BEATRIZ Yo con más celos que[4] iras.
DOÑA ANA No tienes en qué fundarlos,
cuando te aseguro, prima,
que no fue correspondido
de mí tu amante.
CELESTINA Hijas mías,
dejad eso, y ahora vamos
atajando una desdicha

[4] Dialefa entre "que" e "iras".

que va saliendo al camino.
Ya tendréis largas noticias
de mi virtud y mi ciencia,
que, sin ser hipocresía
ni vanidad, decir puedo
que de la negra magía[5]
he apurado los más altos
secretos que su caos[6] cifra;
sin que en el más arduo empeño,
en la ocasión más precisa,
en mi susto haya podido
socorrerme una mentira;
que esto sólo es la verdad,
por mi fe, aunque yo lo diga;
ya visteis en esta casa
ayer tarde, aunque afligidas,
como os libró aquese espejo
de las horrorosas iras
de don Luis,[7] y eso en virtud
de la amada ciencia mía;
pues sabed que esta mañana,
escupiendo airadas hidras,
me dijo, en mi misma cara,
cómo individual noticia
tenía de que don Diego
era amante de su[8] hija;
que sabía que era noble,
y que era traidor sabía,
y, de su casa informado,
también me dijo que iba
a matarle o a casarle;
grandes son ambas desdichas,
pues nunca bien se enlazaron
los amores con las iras;
dijo, en fin, que iba a matarle

[5] Véanse también los vv. 1851, 2101 y 2901 donde se pronunciaba "ma-gí-a".
[6] Sinéresis en "caos".
[7] No presenciaron el embuste ni supieron del engaño del espejo.
[8] Dialefa entre "su" e "hija".

o a que le diese una firma
de ser tu esposo.

DOÑA ANA Detente,
no prosigas, no prosigas,
que antes me daré mil muertes,
porque, ofendiendo a mi prima,
aunque fuera gusto mío
y fuera correspondida
mi voluntad, despreciara* despreciaría
sus finezas y caricias.

DOÑA BEATRIZ Yo te estimo esa atención,
y sabe que quien la estima
quisiera poder cederte
lo mismo que desestimas.

CELESTINA Ea, al remedio acudamos.

DOÑA BEATRIZ Fuerza es que a don Diego escriba
un papel, porque otro medio
no[9] hay, y tú, Celestina,
podrás llevarle.

CELESTINA Eso no,
porque soy muy conocida
de don Luis, y puede acaso
encontrarme, y no querría
malograseis el suceso;
mejor será que Antoñica
le lleve.

DOÑA BEATRIZ Muy bien has dicho;
voy a escribirle. *Vase.*

CELESTINA Ea, aprisa.

DOÑA ANA ¿Si habrá llegado mi padre
a su casa? ¡Ay, Celestina!,
toda el alma se me anega,
y, en congojas repetidas,
el corazón por los ojos
líquido fuego destila.
¡Ay malogrado amor mío!

CELESTINA No te aflijas, no te aflijas,
que según don Luis me dijo,

---

[9] Dialefa entre "no" y "hay".

aun de cierto no sabía
su casa; y confía en mí,
puesto que no se limita
mi ciencia a tan cortos lances,
porque en más arduos estriba;
y así, tenga vida yo,
como de mi peregrina
maña espero que he de hallar
industria, estudio y magía[10]
para hacer . . . pero callemos,
que siempre en la boca misma
parece mal la alabanza,
y no quiero que se diga
de mi virtud y mi ciencia
que lo que ha de hacer publica.

DOÑA ANA Mucho estimo tu fineza.

CELESTINA ([*Aparte*] Mas don Juan a toda prisa
viene por la calle, y juzgo
que hacia acá el paso encamina,
que en la luna deste espejo
le he visto, y no participa
doña Ana, por estar vuelta
de espaldas, desta noticia;
y así, ahora vaya de embuste.)

DOÑA ANA ¿Qué, en fin, dices, Celestina,
que has de hallar industria y arte
con que componer mis dichas?

CELESTINA Sí.[11]

DOÑA ANA Y ¿Cuándo podré ver
a don Juan?

CELESTINA Si tú te animas,
muy presto has de poder verle.
¿Tendrás valor?

DOÑA ANA ¿Que eso digas
a quien ama?

CELESTINA ¿Has de asustarte?

DOÑA ANA No cabe en mí cobardía.

---

[10] Véase la nota del v. 2646.

[11] Dialefa entre "Sí" e "Y".

CELESTINA Pues ánimo.
DOÑA ANA Acaba ya
de darme esta nueva vida.
CELESTINA Pues está atenta a ese espejo
y verás su imagen misma,
y también podrás hablarle,
sin volver la cara, y mira
que guardes este secreto.
DOÑA ANA Que le guardaré confía.
CELESTINA Encárgote que no vuelvas
la cara.
DOÑA ANA Estoy advertida.
CELESTINA ([*Aparte*] Voy a avisar a don Juan,
pues que ya estará acá arriba.) *Vase.*
DOÑA ANA ¿Qué es esto? Yo nada veo,
sino es mi confusión misma.
¿Dónde estás, don Juan? ¿Adónde?

Sale DON JUAN.

DON JUAN Aquí dijo Celestina
que estaba sola doña Ana.
¿Qué es esto? Está divertida
con la imagen de su rostro.
DOÑA ANA ¡Cielos, ya llegó a mi vista!
Ilusión, sombra, fantasma,
¿posible es que necesitas*[12] necesites
de encantos y de ilusiones
para verme? ¡Prima, prima!
DON JUAN ¿De qué nacerá este asombro?

Vase acercando DON JUAN.

DOÑA ANA No te acerques, que me irrita
tu ingratitud aun en sombras.
DON JUAN ¡Ay más rara maravilla!

---

[12] "Necesitas" mantiene la asonancia i-a.

Al paño CELESTINA.

CELESTINA Bien me ha salido este embuste;
si ella vuelve, soy perdida;
mas antes podré sacarle
de aquí, pues la pobrecita
ha tragado aqueste encanto
por su propria golosina.

DOÑA ANA Don Juan, espera, detente,
no te acerques, pues me olvidas.

DON JUAN ¿Cómo podré olvidar yo,
ingrata, crüel, esquiva,
mi lealtad[13] y tu inconstancia,
mi amor y tu tiranía,
cuando en el papel del alma
mi memoria tiene escritas
tu traición y mi fineza,
tu mudanza y mi desdicha,
sirviendo mi voz de pluma,
mi triste llanto de tinta?

DOÑA ANA ¿Qué, en fin, no me has olvidado
por el amor de mi prima?

DON JUAN Dime, ¿y tú a mí, por don Diego,
es cierto que no me olvidas?

DOÑA ANA Yo soy constante.

DON JUAN Yo firme.

DOÑA ANA Yo soy leal y soy fina.

DON JUAN Pues ¿por qué el rostro no vuelves?

DOÑA ANA Por no perder esta dicha.

DON JUAN ¿Qué dicha?

DOÑA ANA De solo verte.

DON JUAN ¿Quién entenderá este enigma?
¿Dónde me traen[14] tus encantos,
engañosa Celestina?
Yo he de apurar tus cautelas.

CELESTINA ¿Oh quién pudiera decirla
que no vuelva acá la cara?

---

[13] Sinéresis de "lealtad".

[14] Sinéresis de "traen".

Pero está tan embebida
que juzgo que será ociosa
diligencia el prevenirla;
quiero a don Juan hacer seña
o llamar con voz remisa.

DON JUAN ¿Quién este encanto ha causado,
su hermosura o mi desdicha?

Vase acercando DON JUAN.

DOÑA ANA No te acerques, que me pierdes
y te pierdo; ya se entibian
mis palabras, porque al labio
salen tan desfallecidas
que parece que respiro
en cada aliento una vida.

Cae desmayada.

DON JUAN ¿Qué es esto, doña Ana?

Sale CELESTINA.

CELESTINA Espera,
que don Luis sube acá arriba.

DON JUAN Dime, ¿qué es esto, traidora,
no ves que el alma rendida
tiene a un desmayo doña Ana?

CELESTINA Véte, porque más peligra
si aquí te encuentra su padre.

DON JUAN ¿Qué importa perder la vida
donde la pierde mi dama?

CELESTINA Por su reputación mira,
que yo te doy la palabra
que la veas bien aprisa
buena y sana, pues yo sé
de qué su mal se origina.

DON JUAN ¿Cuándo, dime, la veré?

CELESTINA Yo prometo que a su vista
vuelvas bien presto, y ahora
por esa escalera arriba

sube, porque deste cuarto
es difícil la salida,
pues la escalera ha subido
ya don Luis.

DON JUAN — Por que* no digas (para que)
que arriesgo su honor, me oculto.

CELESTINA — Señoras, ¡ay tal desdicha!
traed agua, traed agua.

Salen DOÑA BEATRIZ y INES.

INES — Pues ¿qué? ¿Se quema la Villa?

CELESTINA — Doña Ana se ha desmayado,
que las amantes fatigas
la tratan con tal rigor
que, porque ahora divertía
sus pesares con los míos,
quiso amor —¡ah suerte impía—
que un parasismo la diera.

INES — Pues voy por agua bendita.

DOÑA ANA — ¡Jesús me valga!

DOÑA BEATRIZ — Parece
que ya el desaliento anima.

DOÑA ANA — ¿Dónde estás, don Juan? ¿Adónde
te esconden las nieblas frías?

DOÑA BEATRIZ — ¿Qué don Juan?

DOÑA ANA — Yo le hablé en sombras.

DOÑA BEATRIZ — ¿Qué sombras? Vuelve en ti, prima.

DON JUAN — No salgo, por descifrar *Al paño.*
de una vez tantos enigmas;
y por si acaso don Luis,
como dijo Celestina,
está cerca, porque no
percibo señas distintas
desde este sitio.

DOÑA BEATRIZ — Entra dentro
a descansar.

DOÑA ANA — Mal se alivia
una alma bañada en penas.

DOÑA BEATRIZ — Inés, entra con mi prima.

INES — Vamos, pues la casa tiene

dos entradas y salidas.[15] *Va[n]se.*

DOÑA BEATRIZ Dime, ¿cómo fue el desmayo?
¿Qué sombras fueron malignas
estas en que vio a don Juan?

CELESTINA Anda, que fue fantasía
que pintaría su idea.

DOÑA BEATRIZ Dímelo, y esta sortija
toma, en fe de la amistad.

CELESTINA ([*Aparte*] Cayó el pájaro en la liga.)
¿Guardarás secreto?

DOÑA BEATRIZ Sí.

CELESTINA ¿Culparásme?

DOÑA BEATRIZ Soy tu amiga.

CELESTINA Pues oye, en la reflexión
de ese espejo ver quería
a don Juan.

DOÑA BEATRIZ ¿Y llegó a verle?

CELESTINA Sí, y ésa fue su desdicha,
porque no tuvo valor
para hablarle.

DOÑA BEATRIZ Es cobardía
confesar un pecho que ama
y acobardarse en las dichas.

CELESTINA ([*Aparte*] Ya en el mismo espejo miro
a don Diego y Antoñica;
si Beatriz[16] quisiera verle,
me valiera otra sortija;
pues cierto es que me valiera
con la mesma de la misma.)
¿Quieres tú ver a don Diego?

DOÑA BEATRIZ Te estuviera agradecida
con demonstración* el alma. *demostración*

CELESTINA ¿Tendrás valor?

DOÑA BEATRIZ Y osadía.

CELESTINA ¿Sabrás guardarme secreto?

DOÑA BEATRIZ Soy noble, y con él me obligas.

CELESTINA A esa muda reflexión

---

[15] Alusión a *Casa con dos puertas mala es de guardar* de Calderón.

[16] Sinéresis en "Beatriz".

del espejo atenta mira,
y verás cuán sin engaños
te dice, por mi magía,[17]
el estado de don Diego;
y repara que si miras
a otra parte que te pierdes,
que así se perdió tu prima,
quedándose desmayada.

DOÑA BEATRIZ En todo es bien que te siga.

CELESTINA No vuelvas esa cabeza.

DOÑA BEATRIZ No haré.

CELESTINA ([*Aparte*] Ya estará acá arriba;
hoy corren bien mis embustes.) *Vase.*

DOÑA BEATRIZ Celestina, amiga mía,
¿cómo me dejas ahora?
Mas yo allí mi imagen misma
sólo encuentro. ¿Dónde está
el bien que me solicitas?
¿Dónde está don Diego?

Sale DON DIEGO.

DON DIEGO Aquí
dice que entre Celestina;
pero allí a Beatriz[18] encuentro
en su espejo divertida,
que solo él imitar puede
su airosa beldad divina.

DOÑA BEATRIZ ¡Válgame el cielo! El parece;
no es sombra, no es fantasía,
realidad[19] es y evidencia.

DON DIEGO ¿De quién tanto se retira?
¿Por quién serán los extremos?

DOÑA BEATRIZ Más que me templa, me indigna
el verte a la reflexión
de este espejo.

---

[17] Véase la nota del v. 2646.

[18] Sinéresis en "Beatriz".

[19] Sinéresis en "realidad".

DON DIEGO ¡Ah enemiga,
falsa, engañosa sirena,
aspid, basilisco, arpía
que, aunque cuando miras matas,
más cruel eres si no miras!

Al paño DON JUAN.

DON JUAN Don Diego es éste. ¡Ah traidor!
¿Que sus voces no perciba
ni alcance a ver con quién habla?
DOÑA BEATRIZ Véte, don Diego.
DON DIEGO ¡Ah enemiga!
DOÑA BEATRIZ No he de verte; véte, véte,
huye,[20] huye de mi vista,
que, para ver tus traiciones,
basta la memoria mía.
DON DIEGO Pues vuelve el rostro siquiera.
DOÑA BEATRIZ No puedo.
DON DIEGO ¿Por qué me avisas
en un papel de mi riesgo,
si no temes mi rüina?
DOÑA BEATRIZ Por piedad.
DON DIEGO ¿Y la piedad
embozas con la mentira?
DOÑA BEATRIZ Yo no te engaño.
DON DIEGO Eres falsa.
DOÑA BEATRIZ Tú ingrato.
DON DIEGO Tú fementida,
vuelve el rostro.
DOÑA BEATRIZ Ya le vuelvo;
([*Aparte*] mas ¿cómo las ansias mías
no temen el riesgo grave
que me avisó Celestina?
Pues nunca estas cosas pueden
despreciarse, aunque fingidas
parezcan, que en ser verdad
puedo aventurar la vida,

[20] Dialefa entre "huye" y "huye".

y, con tan costoso examen,
no importa que sean[21] mentidas.)

DON DIEGO ¿Es posible que no vuelvas?

DOÑA BEATRIZ Dime, traidor, ¿cómo olvidas
la perla, el ave y la flor?[22]
¿Tú no amas a dos?

DON DIEGO ¡Ah impía!
Ya conozco tus cautelas;
y si acaso Celestina
te ha engañado en ese espejo,
como a mí, en ella mis iras
tomarán justa venganza.

DON LUIS ¡Antonia, Inés! *Dentro.*

DOÑA BEATRIZ ¡Gran desdicha!
Mi tío viene; yo intento
huir; adiós, hasta otro día.

Vase sin volver el rostro.

DON DIEGO Aguarda, tirana, espera [*romances*]

Sale Celestina.

CELESTINA ¿Qué es esto, señor don Diego,
cómo aun os estáis aquí?

DON DIEGO Tu encanto me tiene muerto.

CELESTINA *El encanto es la hermosura,*
que el mío no tiene efecto;
idos.

DON DIEGO Yo te buscaré.

CELESTINA Salgamos de aqueste riesgo
sin que estas damas peligren,
que después ya nos veremos.

DON DIEGO Mira si puedo salir.

CELESTINA Por muy difícil lo tengo,
porque se viene acercando

---

[21] Sinéresis en "sean".

[22] Véanse vv. 2014–46.

hacia nosotros el viejo.
DON DIEGO Pues aquí intento ocultarme.

Vase a esconder donde está DON JUAN.

DON JUAN No puede ser, deteneos.
CELESTINA ¡Perdida soy, que le ha visto!
DON DIEGO ¿Quién aquí osado y resuelto
se esconde?
DON JUAN Quien solo puede;
suspended ahora el acero,
pues ya sé que sois la causa
de mis iras y mis celos,
y hoy he de tomar venganza.
DON DIEGO Pues en Trïana os espero
a las cinco de la tarde,
porque ya informado vengo
de quién sois y que vos fuisteis
el que me hirió; y aunque os debo
la vida, antes el honor
es que el agradecimiento.
CELESTINA ¿Dónde vas?
DON DIEGO Deja que salga.
CELESTINA ¿No oyes a don Luis?
DON DIEGO Mis celos
ni oyen ni miran ni atienden.
CELESTINA Pues yo oigo, miro y atiendo
que tú estás desafïado,
que está ya cerca este viejo,
que estas damas están muertas
y que yo tengo gran miedo.

Dentro DON LUIS.

DON LUIS Di que salgan a esta cuadra.
CELESTINA Por tu vida, evita el riesgo.
DON DIEGO Pues ¿qué he de hacer?
CELESTINA Esconderte,
que mi palabra te empeño
de sacarte, pues bien sabes
que es fácil, habiendo espejos.

DON DIEGO Pues allí está mi enemigo,
aquí don Luis; y así, intento
cubrirme desta cortina,
pues que no hay otro remedio.

Escóndese DON DIEGO.

CELESTINA Ahora salgo a recibirle.

Sale DON LUIS.

DON LUIS Celestina, al tal don Diego
no ha sido fácil hallarle.
CELESTINA ([*Aparte*] Gran mentecato es el viejo,
pues sólo estándose en casa
pudiera encontrarle.) Es cierto
que ya es vana diligencia,
que el amante verdadero
de doña Ana yo he sabido
que no es ése.
DON LUIS ¿Cómo, ¡ay cielos!,
le conoces?
CELESTINA Le conozco,
que en Sevilla es caballero.
DON LUIS Di su nombre.

Sale[n] DOÑA ANA, DOÑA BEATRIZ *y* INES.

DOÑA BEATRIZ ¿Señor?
DOÑA ANA ¿Padre?
DON LUIS Pero después hablaremos.
De mi hermano tengo cartas,
y juzgo que los afectos
pueden darse parabienes
del deseado[23] casamiento.
DOÑA BEATRIZ Y ¿con quién es?
DON LUIS Es, sobrina,
con don Juan Téllez Pacheco,

[23] Sinéresis en "deseado".

deudo nuestro muy cercano.
DOÑA BEATRIZ Yo no me caso con deudos.
DON LUIS ¿Por qué no?
DOÑA BEATRIZ Porque son siempre
desgraciados casamientos.
INES Mucho peor[24] fuera con deudas,
que es como se casan ellas.[25]
DON LUIS Mira que he de responder.
DOÑA ANA Siempre, señor, fue violento
cautivar un albedrío
que le da por libre el cielo.
DON LUIS Pues tú, aleve hija, ¿te opones
al dictamen ni al consejo
de los padres?
DOÑA ANA Siendo injustos,
—bien que nunca los desprecio—
no los sigo.
DOÑA BEATRIZ Mi albedrío
a nadie ha de estar sujeto. *Vase.*
DON LUIS Y tú, ¿qué eliges?
DOÑA ANA Yo sólo
elijo el irme a un convento. *Vase.*
DON LUIS ¡Ay resolución más libre!
CELESTINA Bien sé yo de qué nace esto.
DON LUIS ¿De qué nace?
CELESTINA De lo mismo
que te dije.
DON LUIS No te entiendo;
di, ¿a quién mi[26] hija se inclina,
quién es?
CELESTINA Señor, no me atrevo
a decirlo, porque yo
soy mujer honrada, y tengo
la amistad y la palabra
empeñada en el secreto.
DON LUIS Pues de aquí no has de salir

[24] Sinéresis en "peor".
[25] "Ellas" destruye la asonancia e-o.
[26] Dialefa entre "mi" e "hija".

sin decirlo, o, ¡vive el cielo!,
que rompa puerta esta daga
en tu pecho aleve.

CELESTINA Quedo,
que si en el pecho me das,
puedes romperme el secreto.

DON LUIS Dilo, traidora.

CELESTINA Si aquí
te contentaras con verlos,
te mostrara los amantes
de tu hija y sobrina.

DON LUIS El medio
no era malo por ahora,
que, después de conocerlos,
yo los supiera buscar;
pero di, ¿quién* son? quiénes

CELESTINA No puedo.

DON LUIS Dilo, acaba.

CELESTINA Es imposible;
no hay sino matarme luego,
que no es fácil el morirme,
si yo matarme no quiero.

DON LUIS Pues ¿cómo sabré quién son?

CELESTINA Volviendo el rostro a ese espejo,
pues que no es la vez primera.

DON LUIS ([*Aparte*] De aquesta mujer contemplo
en cada voz un prodigio,
en cada acción un portento:
¡mujer rara y peregrina!)
En fin, ¿el mudo reflejo *A ella.*
representará su imagen?

CELESTINA Sí.

DON LUIS ¿De los dos?

CELESTINA Los dos mesmos.

DON LUIS El de Beatriz[27] quiero ver.

CELESTINA Pues está, don Luis, atento
y sin moverte.

DON LUIS Ya lo hago.

---

[27] Sinéresis en "Beatriz".

CELESTINA Pues yo a conjurar empiezo.

Llégase donde está DON DIEGO.

Idos presto, pues que veis
que no ha podido otro medio
valerme.

DON DIEGO Saldré, por sólo
averiguar tus enredos.

CELESTINA ([*Aparte*] Quien mirare aqueste encanto
verá que esto no es más que esto.)

DON LUIS No veo[28] nada.

CELESTINA No te muevas,
que ya llega. ([*Aparte*] Idos, don Diego,
pues don Luis cree que es encanto.)

DON LUIS Ya le admiro, ya le veo.

DON DIEGO Por buscar a mi enemigo,
tus embustes agradezco. *Vase.*

CELESTINA Después te satisfaré.

DON LUIS Aguarda, traidor don Diego;
¿dónde estás?

CELESTINA Si el rostro vuelves,
¿no era preciso el perderlo?

DON LUIS ([*Aparte*] Véngueme el cielo de ti,
aleve, mal caballero.)
Este, dime, ¿no es el mismo
que vi la otra vez?

CELESTINA Es cierto.

DON LUIS Luego ¿tú me has engañado?

CELESTINA No engañé, pues tu deseo
quiso saber quién hablaba
por la reja, y fue don Diego
entonces, como es ahora.

DON LUIS Dime, esotro caballero,
¿podré verle?

CELESTINA Y aun hablarle,
si estás menos descompuesto,
mirando la reflexión.

---

[28] Sinéresis en "veo".

DON LUIS Pues yo estaré atento.
CELESTINA Oh tú, que del negro abismo
las gargantas del Cerbero★[29] Cancerbero
pasaste. ([*Aparte a* DON JUAN] Señor don Juan,
doña Ana os pide que luego
salgáis de su casa, porque★ para que
la saquéis de un grave riesgo.)
DON JUAN Quien hablaba en esta sala,
¿no era su padre?
CELESTINA Sí, el viejo
que con un encanto de ojos
tiene un mortal embeleso;
y aunque le encuentres, no atiendas
a su voz ni a sus extremos.
DON JUAN Nada hasta ahora he percebido,
con estar tan cerca.
CELESTINA Luego
te diré cuánto ha pasado.
DON LUIS Ver a este amante deseo.
DON JUAN Por buscar a mi enemigo,
aun más puntual te obedezco.

Va pasando DON JUAN.

DON LUIS ¿Este no es don Juan de Lara?
Tente, aguarda.

Detiénese DON JUAN, *y* CELESTINA *le hace señas que se vaya.*

CELESTINA Véte presto.
DON JUAN ¿Cómo, cielos, no me sigue,
si me ve por el espejo?
CELESTINA Véte, véte.
DON JUAN Absorto voy
de ver prodigio tan nuevo.
DON LUIS ¡Ah traidor, aleve amigo!
Ya ni su imagen encuentro.

---

[29] Perro de tres cabezas que guarda la entrada a los Infiernos.

¿Celestina?

CELESTINA ¿Qué me quieres?

DON LUIS Deja que vaya tras ellos.

CELESTINA Pues, ¿dónde, di, has de encontrarlos?

DON LUIS Dices bien, que este fue un sueño,
una ilusión, una sombra,
un deshonor, un tormento.

CELESTINA Yo lo que hacen te dijera,
y donde están, pero temo
—como soy tan desgraciada—
que reveles el secreto.

DON LUIS No haré, y ahora estos escudos
toma en agradecimiento.

CELESTINA Vivas mil años, y aguarda,
porque en ese mismo espejo
lo he de ver, que pues hay arte
para otros, yo soy primero.

Mirando al espejo CELESTINA.

DON LUIS ([*Aparte*] ¡Qué tal ciencia deposite
Dios en vaso tan pequeño,
tan frágil, tan quebradizo!
¡Oh sumos altos secretos,
pues, aun siendo inescrutables,
os reveláis en misterios!)

Habla mirando al espejo CELESTINA.

CELESTINA En fin, vos, señor don Juan,
¿decís que al señor don Diego
le lleváis desafiado
a Trïana?

DON LUIS ¿Qué es aquesto?

CELESTINA No es más de lo que has oído.

DON LUIS ¿A Trïana van?

CELESTINA Es cierto.

DON LUIS ¿Sabes a qué hora?

CELESTINA A las cinco,
y ahora, poco más o menos,
son las cuatro.

DON LUIS — Pues yo voy
a esperarlos.
CELESTINA — No tan presto.
DON LUIS — No pide más dilación. *[Vase.]*
CELESTINA — Véte, pues; mamóla el viejo;
ahora veamos[30] estas damas,
que estarán con gran deseo
de saber aquestos lances
o estos encantos. Oh ingenio,
si hay tontos que te acrediten,
¿qué te importa el no haber hecho
fatigar de los estantes
el polvo, si es su desvelo
sólo para sacudir
la dulce quietud del sueño?
Y si la fama consiste
en ajena opinión, cierto
que hará mal de no dormir
quien supiere estos enredos
tan fáciles, tan sin ciencia,
tan sin arte y sin ingenio,
que los llega a autorizar
la opinión de un majadero.

Salen DOÑA ANA, DOÑA BEATRIZ, ANTONIA y INES.

DOÑA ANA — ¿Qué te haces aquí tan sola?
CELESTINA — Estaba mirando a Venus,[31]
que se halla de oposición
con Marte, aquel dios sangriento.
DOÑA BEATRIZ — Y ¿qué indica?
CELESTINA — Un gran disturbio
entre amantes, pues la encuentro
mirar de trino,[32] pasando

---

[30] Sinéresis en "ahora" y "veamos".

[31] "Venus" no rompe la asonancia e-o.

[32] *Trino*—"En la Astronomia es el aspecto, que se considera entre dos Planetas, quando distan entre sí ciento y veinte grados: esto es, quando segun sus longitudes se refieren à dos puntos de la Ecliptica distantes entre sí ciento y veinte grados, ò un tercio de círculo" (*Aut.*).

a la sexta casa;[33] y luego
el mismo Marte la mira
con raro, infeliz aspecto.

DOÑA ANA Yo no entiendo astrología.

CELESTINA ([*Aparte*] Pues yo tampoco la entiendo,
y, en el modo de decirlo,
pudierais bien conocerlo,
a tener cortas noticias.)

DOÑA ANA Dime, ¿y los amantes nuestros
corren peligro?

CELESTINA Y muy grande,
pues, según me avisa el cielo,
ahora están desafiados
don Diego y don Juan.

DOÑA BEATRIZ ¿Don Diego?

CELESTINA Sí, mas puede ser . . .

Sale MUÑOZ asustado.

MUÑOZ Señoras,
¡gran susto, gran mal, gran riesgo,
gran dolor!

DOÑA ANA ¿Qué traes,[34] Muñoz?

MUÑOZ Traigo sobre mí un gran peso.

CELESTINA Echate ya con la carga,
pues eres tan gran jumento.

MUÑOZ No muy grande, Celestina,
soy tu amigo verdadero;
y sabrás, por que* lo creas, para que
que fui[35] a Tacón siguiendo
en casa del asistente;[36]
preguntéle qué era aquello,

---

[33] *Casa*—"Segun los Astrólogos es una de las cinco dignidades essenciales que Ptholoméo dá à los Planétas: y es un lugár en que hallándose el Planéta se dice hace mayores, y con mas eficacia sus efectos que en otro qualquiera lugár: y assi llaman à Sagitário Casa diurna dé Júpiter, Táuro casa nocturna de Venus" (*Aut.*).

[34] Sinéresis en "traes".

[35] Dialefa entre "fui" y "a".

[36] *Asistente*—"En Sevilla se dá este título y nombre al Corregidór de aquella Ciudad. Tambien los hai en otras partes, como en Santiago y Marchéna, aunque de inferiór representación" (*Aut.*).

y dijo que a delatarte
iba, porque tus enredos
le imputaron de ladrón,
para quitarle el dinero;
despidióseme enojado,
y, aguardando un breve tiempo,
veo salir la justicia
muy armada, y también veo
que llegaron a tu casa
codiciosos y soberbios
una tropa de corchetes* alguaciles
y un caudillo fariseo[37]
que en altas voces decían,
por Trïana discurriendo:
"¿Dónde está aquesta hechicera
encantadora del pueblo?"
Mira si es para temido,
Celestina, este suceso.

CELESTINA Dime, ¿entraron en mi casa?

MUÑOZ No, aunque llamaron muy recio
y por todo el barrio andaban.

DOÑA ANA ¡Gran desdicha!

CELESTINA ¡Ay santos cielos!
Aquí dio fin Celestina
y todo su encantamiento.

ANTONIA ¡Qué bien parecerá ahorcada!

INES Ya está ensayando los gestos.

DOÑA BEATRIZ ¿Qué hemos de hacer si descubren
que estás aquí?

CELESTINA Irme[38] huyendo.

DOÑA ANA Eso no, estando en mi casa,
que yo ampararte deseo,
y ahora, a discurrir vamos
del desafío, si es cierto.

CELESTINA Para embarazarlo ya
se me ha ofrecido un buen medio.

---

[37] *Fariseo*—"Por semejanza se llama el sugéto injusto, cruél, inhumáno, ù horrible de aspecto, y que no se compadece de los trabajos y calamidades ajénas" (*Aut.*).

[38] Dialefa entre "Irme" y "huyendo".

DOÑA BEATRIZ ¿Cuál es?
CELESTINA Después lo sabréis,[39]
que aun no sé si será bueno;
prevenid tinta y papel.
ANTONIA Ya lo está.
DOÑA BEATRIZ Sin alma aliento.
DOÑA ANA ¿Hasta cuándo, cruel fortuna,
durará tu horrible ceño? *Vase.*
DOÑA BEATRIZ ¿Hasta cuándo, amor injusto,
has de ser tirano y ciego? *Vase.*
CELESTINA ¿Hasta cuándo, embustes míos,
duraréis, porque ya os temo?
MUÑOZ ¿Hasta cuándo has de ser falsa?
INES ¿Y hasta cuándo tú grosero?
ANTONIA Hasta cuando yo quisiere.
MUÑOZ El cuando al fin le veremos.

Vanse entrando cada uno con sus versos,
y sale[n] DON JUAN y DON DIEGO.

CUADRO III

DON DIEGO Don Juan, aunque agradecido[40]
pudiera estar, yo confieso
que, si en nobles pechos lidian
dos tan contrarios afectos,
acuerda el honor el odio
y no el agradecimiento.
DON JUAN Yo ahora os quiero vengativo,
y no agradecido os quiero;
pues si atento vuestra vida
defendí que fue, sospecho,
guardárosla por entonces
para quitárosla luego:

---

[39] Celestina piensa avisar a la justicia del desafío por medio de Muñoz.

[40] Los vv. 3289–3333 se parecen al acto primero de *El encanto sin encanto*; vv. 3084–3164 del final de sor Juana no tienen tanto en común con esta comedia de Calderón como el de Vera Tassis.

y así, reñid. *Riñen.*
DON DIEGO Será sólo
con la espada de los celos.
DON JUAN Valiente sois.
DON DIEGO Vos me honráis,
por ser enemigo vuestro.
DON JUAN Herido estoy en la mano.
DON DIEGO ¿Qué queréis hacer?
DON JUAN Yo quiero
mataros.
DON DIEGO Para reñir,
poneos ese pañuelo.

Dale un pañuelo.

DON JUAN Corrido estoy.

Sale DON LUIS.

DON LUIS Aquí están;
mucho de hallaros me[41] huelgo.
DON JUAN A mí me pesa, por que* porque
venganza tomar no puedo.
DON LUIS Y pues la espada en la mano
tenéis, irritado vengo
a mataros a ambos juntos
o uno a uno, cuerpo a cuerpo.
DON JUAN Pues, señor don Luis, ¿la causa
no nos diréis?
DON LUIS El acero
solo os sabrá responder.
DON JUAN Dejad concluir este duelo,
que luego os responderé.
DON LUIS Yo os mataré ahora.
DON DIEGO Teneos,

[41] Dialefa entre "me" y "huelgo".

Pónese al lado de DON JUAN.

que al lado de mi enemigo
me habéis de hallar.

DON LUIS — Eso intento, *Acomete.*
que ambos me habéis ofendido,
y a los dos juntos resuelto
he de matar.

DON JUAN — Eso no.

Pónese DON JUAN al lado de DON LUIS.

Suspended, señor don Diego,
la espada, que es gran ventaja
la nuestra, y yo solo intento
morir a su lado.

DON LUIS — Y yo
no admitir el lado vuestro,
y así me pondré neutral
contra los dos.

Pónese en medio de los dos. Sale TACON.

TACON — Caballeros,
ved que llega la justicia.

DON JUAN — ¿Qué dices?

TACON — Esto es lo cierto,
que en busca de Celestina
andan locos y sangrientos
más de cuarenta corchetes.

DON LUIS — Pues por ahora estén suspensos
nuestros duelos, por no dar
motivo para otros duelos.[42]

DON DIEGO — Envainemos, pues ya llegan.

DON JUAN — Mucho el embarazo siento.

[42] Antanaclasis o juego de palabras basado en "duelos".

Salen los alguaciles.

ALGUACIL 1 Buenas tardes, reyes míos.
TODOS Buenas tardes, caballeros.
ALGUACIL 2 Daos a prisión.
DON JUAN ¿Por qué?
ALGUACIL 1 Porque sabemos de cierto
que venís desafiados.
DON LUIS Muy mal informe es el vuestro,
pues los tres somos amigos.
ALGUACIL 1 Por si acaso es o no cierto,
quedaréis, señor don Luis,
ahora en vuestra casa preso,
adonde nos daréis cuenta
de aquestos dos caballeros.
DON JUAN Yo es forzoso que le siga.
DON DIEGO Los dos le acompañaremos.
ALGUACIL 1 Vamos, que aquesta hechicera
no se ha de escapar.
ALGUACIL 2 Podemos
aquí quedarnos algunos.
ALGUACIL 1 Quedad diligentes, puesto
que ella a casa ha de venir;
vamos.
DON LUIS Vamos, ([*Aparte*] que yo intento
o que allí los dos se casen
o que de allí salgan muertos.) *Vanse.*

CUADRO IV

Salen DOÑA ANA, DOÑA BEATRIZ, CELESTINA, ANTONIA y INES.

CELESTINA Juzgo que ésta es buena industria,
y así, fiarla no quiero
de otro ingenio que del mío.
DOÑA ANA Pues anda y no pierdas tiempo.
CELESTINA Adiós.
DOÑA BEATRIZ Mira por tu vida,
que vas expuesta a gran riesgo,

estando allí la justicia.
CELESTINA Aun no conoces mi ingenio.

Vase CELESTINA.

DOÑA BEATRIZ Mas conozco tus encantos.
DOÑA ANA ¿Qué, en fin, dices que al espejo
pudiste a don Diego ver?
DOÑA BEATRIZ Sí, doña Ana, y aun no creo
que alcance su ciencia a tanto.
DOÑA ANA Prima, yo digo lo mesmo,
porque juzgo que a don Juan
le tenía allí encubierto,
y estar rendida al desmayo
fue causa para no verlo;
que, como yo la creí
al principio, tuve miedo
y no volví la cabeza.
DOÑA BEATRIZ Pues a mí me dijo luego
que, porque tú la volvistes,
te desmayaste.
DOÑA ANA Es incierto.

Sale CELESTINA.

CELESTINA Ay, señoras, —¡gran desdicha!—
la justicia —¡piedad, cielos!—
encontré en aquesta calle,
y al punto me conocieron,
porque siguiéndome vienen.
DOÑA ANA ¿Para cuándo es el ingenio?
DOÑA BEATRIZ Para poder deslumbrarlos,
¿no tienes aquí el espejo?

Salen los ALGUACILES, TACON, DON LUIS, DON JUAN, DON DIEGO y MUÑOZ.

ALGUACIL Daos[43] a prisión, Celestina;

[43] Sinéresis en "Daos".

perdone vuestro respeto,
que este es orden superior.
DOÑA ANA Pues observadle, diciendo
la causa de su prisión.
ALGUACIL Por sus embustes y enredos.
TACON Y porque es una borracha
que a mí, porque soy manchego,
me ha tratado de ladrón,[44]
quitándome mi dinero
con cautelas, con encantos
y con esto y con aquello.
CELESTINA Señor don Luis, socorredme,
pues que ya a Tacón le vuelvo
sus escudos.
TACON Ved no se huya.
ALGUACIL Agarradla.
DOÑA ANA Caballeros,
yo os suplico que os templéis,
si acaso pueden los ruegos
de las damas con vosotros.
ALGUACIL 1 Yo los tengo por preceptos;
decid que dé su descargo.
TACON Mirad que con sus enredos
se ha de escapar.
CELESTINA Yo en mi vida
tuve ciencia ni la tengo,
porque sólo he aprendido
unos embustes caseros
con que, embobando la gente,
fama de astróloga adquiero.
TACON Saber que por una dama
se ausentó y por unos celos,
mi amo don Juan, y que el día
de San Clemente el suceso
sucedió, y ¿saberlo todo
no es hechicería?[45]

---

[44] Herrero García no menciona esta característica de ladrón entre las enumeradas por él como perteneciente a los manchegos. Véanse pp. 198–201.

[45] Sinéresis en "hechicería".

CELESTINA Pues necio,
¿qué hechizo en eso haber puede,
si vino a ese mismo tiempo
doña Ana y me contó el caso?
Yo, por formar el enredo,
pregunté las circunstancias;
acaeció el venir luego
don Juan, contarle lo mismo
que había oído y don Juan creerlo;
¿no es verdad esto, señora?

DOÑA ANA Sí, que negarlo no puedo.

TACON Dime, ¿tú no adivinaste,
con hechizos o embelecos,
que mi amo venía a España
de Flandes, porque violento,
a la fuerza de un conjuro
tuyo, de allá vino, haciendo
que todas estas señoras
se aprovechasen del miedo
para huir dél?

CELESTINA También es falso,
que él vino por su pie mesmo
a traer de Flandes cartas
al señor don Luis.

DON JUAN Es cierto.

CELESTINA Y yo, como antes le oí
en mi casa todo el cuento,
con arte dije a doña Ana
que le vería muy presto;
llegó, y también vio a Beatriz,[46]
que estaba aquí al mismo tiempo;
con que allí hizo su hermosura
el encanto y no mi ingenio.

DON JUAN *Más encanto es la hermosura*,[47]
dices bien, yo lo confieso.

INES ¿Y cómo, di, a mi señora
enseñaste en el espejo

---

[46] Sinéresis en "Beatriz".

[47] Título de una una comedia de Juan Bautista Diamante.

a don Diego?
ANTONIA Y mi ama,[48]
¿cómo en sus claros reflejos
vio a don Juan?
CELESTINA Estad atentas,
veréis cómo no hay en eso
hechizo alguno: mirad
a la reflexión del mesmo
espejo y decid: ¿quién pasa
por la calle ahora?
TACON Un cochero.
CELESTINA ¿Y ahora quién va?
ANTONIA Una dama.
CELESTINA ¿Y ahora?
MUÑOZ Un burro.
CELESTINA ¿Y ahora?
INES Un perro.[49]
CELESTINA Pues mirad qué fácil ciencia;
doña Ana y Beatriz vuelto
tenían[50] el rostro hacia mí;
y yo, mirando al espejo,
vi que don Juan entró en casa
y, de allí a poco, don Diego,
y, diciéndolo a las dos,
por encanto lo creyeron.
DON LUIS Pues la sombra que yo vi
en el mismo cristal terso,
¿no fue hechicería?
CELESTINA No,
dígalo el señor don Diego
que dos veces escondido
estuvo aquí, y vos, creyendo
que era en virtud de mi ciencia,
le dejasteis ir.
DON DIEGO Es cierto
que yo salí, y fue admirando

[48] Dialefa entre "Diego" e "y" y entre "mi" y "ama".
[49] Habrá sinéresis sólo la primera vez que se dice "ahora".
[50] Sinéresis en "tenían".

más su engaño que el portento.
DON LUIS Corrido estoy, vive Dios;
y en ese mudo reflejo
¿a don Juan no vi también?
DON JUAN También yo estaba aquí dentro.
DON LUIS Pues ¿cómo, aleves y osados,
en mi casa . . . ?

Va a sacar la espada.

ALGUACIL Deteneos,
que está la justicia aquí.
DON LUIS Pues ¿cómo mi honor, soberbios,
intentáis así manchar?
DOÑA ANA No le mancha, y, si hizo[51] esto,
fue por ser esposo mío.
DON LUIS Dale la mano.
DON JUAN La aceto* acepto
con el alma y con la vida,
seguro ya de mis celos.
DON LUIS ¿Y vos?
DOÑA BEATRIZ También es mi esposo;
ésta es mi mano, don Diego.
DON DIEGO Feliz ha sido mi suerte.
DON JUAN También yo dárosla quiero,
pues, si yo os herí, me heristeis,
con que se concluye el duelo.
DON LUIS Quede hoy libre Celestina,
por que* los júbilos nuestros para que
se celebren sin azar,
que yo daros os prometo
los cien escudos, quedando
todo este caso en secreto.[52]
ALGUACIL Viváis, señor, muchos años.
CELESTINA Yo también os lo agradezco.
([*Aparte*] Lo que dura una comedia

[51] Dialefa entre "si" e "hizo".

[52] En los trances y casos de honor, el guardar silencio (no divulgar públicamente lo que aconteció) es una obligación de todo noble, lección clara de *No hay cosa como callar* de Calderón.

dicen que dura un enredo;[53]
y así, ahora pienso vengarme
de Tacón.) Señor, yo os ruego
que ahora me hagáis justicia
con este infame embustero,
por que* cumpla una palabra. para que
TACON ¿Cuál es?
CELESTINA La de casamiento,
que tú mil veces me has dado,
y has fingido estos enredos,
por no llegar a cumplirla.
TACON Sólo me faltaba[54] esto;
bruja, hechicera, ¿yo a ti?
Arredro vayas, arredro.[55]
CELESTINA Haced justicia, señores.
ALGUACIL Si esto es así, casaos[56] luego
o iréis conmigo a la cárcel.
TACON Ved que es falso.
CELESTINA Vaya preso,
que tengo dos mil testigos.
ALGUACIL Casaos.
TACON ¿No hay otro medio?
ALGUACIL No
TACON ¿Ello ha de ser?
ALGUACIL Luego al punto.
TACON Pues yo me caso, advirtiendo
que puedo probar la fuerza
siempre.[57]
CELESTINA Pues ahora no quiero
casarme con quien engaña
a dos mujeres a un tiempo.

---

53 *Enredo*—Juego de palabras basado en una dilogía: 1) intriga dramática y 2) mentira o engaño.

54 Dialefa entre "faltaba" y "esto".

55 *Arredro*—"Equivále à atrás, ù detrás, ò hácia atrás. Usase de ordinário como cierto género de conjúro, para ahuyentar ò hacer retirar à alguno. Es vulgar, y regularmente vá acompañado con la palabra vayas" (*Aut.*).

56 Sinéresis en "casaos".

57 Alusión a un impedimento en el proyectado casamiento que resultaría en su anulación.

TACON ¿A quién?
CELESTINA A mí y a Antoñica.
TACON Díganlo estos caballeros
si yo en toda la comedia
la hablé palabra.
CELESTINA En secreto,
entre jornada y jornada
la enamoraste.
TACON Sí, es cierto,
ésta es, Antonia, mi mano.
ANTONIA Estos son mis cinco dedos.
MUÑOZ Inés, cásate conmigo.
INES Sin enamorarme, aceto.
DON JUAN ¡Válgate Dios por encantos!
DON DIEGO ¡Válgate Dios por enredos!
CELESTINA *El encanto es la hermosura.*
DON JUAN Es verdad.
DON DIEGO Así lo creo.
CELESTINA *El hechizo sin hechizo*
le llamaréis.
ANA Y BEATRIZ Yo lo apruebo.
CELESTINA Ya aquí, señores, da fin
la Celestina a su enredo.
Y don Juan de Vera os pide
perdón del atreviemiento
de acabar una comedia
de tan superior ingenio;
pues lo[58] hizo motivado
de un soberano decreto,
y por confirmar que es sólo
El mejor amigo el muerto.[59]

---

[58] Dialefa entre "lo" e "hizo".
[59] Alusión a una comedia de Calderón en colaboración.

LA CONCLUSION ANONIMA (ATRIBUIDA A SOR JUANA)

CUADRO II

Sale[n] DOÑA ANA y DOÑA BEATRIZ

[*redondillas*]

DOÑA ANA De buen empeño salimos.
DOÑA BEATRIZ ¿Qué importa de uno salgamos
si en otro mayor quedamos?
Pues por lo menos supimos
que don Diego de Guevara
es el que a entrambas quería.
DOÑA ANA Con buena sofistería
quiso decir que era rara
fineza el servir a dos.
DOÑA BEATRIZ Un amante convencido,
tarde o nunca, se ha valido
de mejor disculpa.
DOÑA ANA ¡Ay Dios!
Aunque no es buena, la oyera
yo de don Juan, siendo a quien
sé que a ti te quiere bien.
DOÑA BEATRIZ Si ese tu consuelo fuera,
¿no es mejor oír de mí
que yo no le quiero a él?,
con que ese temor crüel
cesará.
DOÑA ANA Si eso es así,
que el verle de otra despreciado[1]
una a su amante, es consuelo,
pierde, Beatriz,[2] el recelo
que a ti don Diego te ha dado

[1] Verso de nueve sílabas.
[2] Sinéresis en "Beatriz" aquí y por todo este final.

conmigo, pues a saber
llegas que le aborrecí,
y tómale para ti,
que yo no le he menester.

DOÑA BEATRIZ Bien argüirte pudiera,
pero no es ésta ocasión
de reducir a cuestión
nuestros celos, y pues fuera
perder tiempo en argüirlos
sin cuidar de remediarlos,
pensemos cómo atajallos
y al mejor fin reducillos.[3]

DOÑA ANA No sé, que a mi padre no
me atreveré a declarar
cuando él me trata casar
en Cádiz.[4]

DOÑA BEATRIZ Tampoco yo
sé cómo explicarme pueda.

Sale MUÑOZ.

MUÑOZ Gracias al cielo que puedo,
señora, hablarte sin miedo,
viendo que tu padre queda
fuera de casa.

DOÑA ANA Muñoz,
¿qué quieres?

MUÑOZ Hay grande mal.

DOÑA BEATRIZ ¿Cómo?

MUÑOZ Es suceso fatal.[5]

DOÑA ANA Dínosle*, pues. Dínoslo.

MUÑOZ Más veloz
que un caballo a Tacón vi
subir esa calle arriba,

---

[3] La rima de la redondilla es incorrecta. En BNM1 cada verso termina en -rlos. En BNM2 hay "remediallos," y el resto sigue a CH.

[4] El padre de doña Beatriz piensa casarla en Cádiz. Véanse vv. 1014–15 y 1403–1405.

[5] Cada edición tiene "Como es suceso fatal". Puesto que tal verso sería un decasílabo, omito "Como".

y que hacia las casas iba
del asistente; advertí[6]
seguirle, y de su cuidado
le pregunté la ocasión,
y con notable aflicción
me contó como había estado
por su mal esta mañana
en casa de Celestina,
y que la vieja maligna,
que siempre a hacer mal se allana,
no contenta con la joya
que en tu casa le quitó,
segunda vez se la armó★ fraguó
con una nueva tramoya★. enredo
Y, sin poder resistillo,
le quitó por sus pecados
cien escudos regalados,
que llevaba en un bolsillo
y tú le diste; y así,
por vengarse de su afrenta,
iba volando a dar cuenta
luego a la justicia[7] y
delatarla de hechicera;
también me dijo que, cuando
estaban los dos voceando[8]
sobre esta nueva quimera,
tu padre entró.

DOÑA ANA ¿Quién?

MUÑOZ Don Luis
tu padre.

DOÑA ANA ¡Ay Dios! ¿A qué iría?

MUÑOZ No sé, que sólo decía
Tacón que estuvo en un tris★ peligro inminente
de entregarle a la justicia
por ladrón, mas que escapó,
y tu padre se quedó

---

[6] *Advertí*—Uso raro del verbo que parece decir "conseguí".
[7] Dialefa entre "justicia" e "y".
[8] Sinéresis en "voceando".

allá, con esta noticia;
y, viendo que no he podido
hacer que deje Tacón
tan grave resolución,
a contártela he venido,
por ver si puedes hacer
que se evite este disgusto
y se se le excuse este susto
a aquella pobre mujer.
Y si gustas, desde aquí
la iré volando a avisar,
antes que pueda llegar
allá Tacón.

DOÑA ANA ¡Ay de mí!,
prima, que en riesgo notable [*romances*]
nos hallamos, pues supuesto
que en casa de Celestina
ha estado mi padre, es cierto
que se puede originar
grave daño.

DOÑA BEATRIZ No es aqueso
lo peor, que quizá iría
a hablar en lo del espejo,
que no nos quiso decir
Celestina;[9] y yo más temo,
que si Tacón ha avisado
a la justicia, debemos
recelar que, si la prenden,
nuestro honor corre gran riesgo,
esparciendo por Sevilla
el rumor del vulgo ciego,
de Celestina el delito
y de las dos el secreto;[10]
porque en semejantes casos
donde el pueblo es juez severo
de culpa y disculpa, siempre

---

[9] Véanse los vv. 2655–60 de VT. Sor Juana aclara aquí que las damas no supieron nada de la traza del espejo.

[10] Véase la nota al v. 3520 de VT.

lo peor elige el pueblo.
DOÑA ANA Pues el peligro en que estamos
nos impide que tratemos
de nuestro amor, porque[11] es
el peligro lo primero,
dejemos ya la porfía
que causó nuestros recelos,
que en las lides amorosas
y en las cuestiones de afectos
se malogra el tiempo cuando
se necesita del tiempo:
y más cuando la ocasión
nos llama a mayor empeño.
Y así, Beatriz, discurramos
el ocurrir a este riesgo,
antes que la dilación
dañe.
DOÑA BEATRIZ Pues el mejor medio
es que las dos disfrazadas,
sin que pueda conocernos
nadie, a ver a Celestina
vamos★. vayamos
DOÑA ANA Repare tu ingenio
los inconvenientes que
nacen, pues que lo primero
peligra nuestra decencia
en ese traje, advirtiendo
que la casa es sospechosa,
como el traje.
DOÑA BEATRIZ Para[12] eso
está la respuesta fácil,
pues ya sabes no son nuevos
los disfraces en Sevilla.
MUÑOZ Y más, señora, sabiendo
que puede pasar muy bien
con máscara de pretexto,
por travesura del gusto,

[11] Dialefa entre "porque" y "es".
[12] Dialefa entre "Para" y "eso".

la necesidad del riesgo.
Y así dice bien tu prima.
DOÑA BEATRIZ No es dudable.
DOÑA ANA Pues yo quiero
que sea[13] fácil como dices
el tomar disfraces; pero
de ir a ver a Celestina,
¿qué logro sacar podemos?
DOÑA BEATRIZ Lo que a tu padre le dijo
saber, y también sabremos
si receló nuestro amor,
si a don Diego ha descubierto.
Dirémosla que Tacón,
por los pasados encuentros,
va a dar cuenta a la justicia
por vengarse; y para[14] eso
la diremos que se oculte,
y aunque parece que es esto,
de Muñoz fiar se puede
como es también nuestro intento
el que nos ofrezca[15] ella
algún mañoso consejo
de su prudencia o su[16] arte
para salir de este empeño;
es preciso que nosotras
vamos*, y, en este supuesto, vayamos
¿qué importa por lo que es más
aventurar lo que es menos?
DOÑA ANA Tu consejo, prima, estimo,
y por que* veas que luego para que
ejecuto lo que dices,
vamos para que, al momento,
Antonia disponer pueda
para los disfraces nuestros
sayas y mantos cerrados;

---

[13] Sinéresis en "sea".
[14] Dialefa entre "para" y "eso".
[15] Dialefa entre "ofrezca" y "ella".
[16] Dialefa entre "su" y "arte".

tú, Muñoz, pues el secreto
sabes, puedes a tu[17] amo
avisarle por que* a un tiempo para que
a Tacón busque. *Vanse.*

CUADRO III

Paséase MUÑOZ.

MUÑOZ Está bien.
Pero he menester primero
discurrir con mucho espacio.
¿Dónde le hallaré muy presto?

Sale DON DIEGO.

DON DIEGO Notablemente confuso
de ayer me tiene el suceso,
sin poder averiguar
la causa de su misterio;
dejo aparte el que, otra vez
volviendo a Sevilla, vuelvo
a ser mariposa amante,
de doña Ana a los reflejos;
bien es verdad que más tibios
de amor los rayos, habiendo
visto de doña Beatriz
la hermosura, cuyo incendio
en el pecho se introdujo
dulce, logrando mi afecto
en Beatriz siempre favores,
siempre en doña Ana desprecios.
También dejo el que fui a verla
a su casa, donde encuentro
a doña Beatriz con ella,
quedando las dos a un tiempo

---

[17] Dialefa entre "tu" y "amo".

ofendidas de mi amor,
como de mi atrevimiento.
Que vino después su padre,
y que yo, a su honor atento
y de sus ruegos instado,
me hube de esconder; mas esto
no es del caso, y solamente
lo que me tiene suspenso
es el que, estando don Luis
allí, pudiese hallar medio
de sacarme Celestina
con la traza del espejo.
Y que viéndome salir
don Luis de su cuarto mesmo,
no habló palabra ni[18] hizo
aun el menor movimiento,
divertido con la imagen
mía que vio en su reflejo:
casa parece de encanto;
ya me es preciso saberlo
para saber si quedó
de mí con algún recelo.
A casa de Celestina
quiero[19] ir, pero allí veo
al crïado de don Juan
de Lara; llamarle quiero:
ah hidalgo.

MUÑOZ ¿Es a mí, señor?

DON DIEGO Sí, que a vuestro amo deseo
ver, que estoy agradecido
de aquel pasado suceso
donde le debí la vida
a su espada y a su esfuerzo.

MUÑOZ Mi amo es caballero andante
que anda desfaciendo tuertos.[20]

DON DIEGO Yo le deseo servir.

[18] Dialefa entre "ni" e "hizo".
[19] Dialefa entre "quiero" e "ir".
[20] Alusión obvia al *Quijote*.

¿Sabéis dónde está?
MUÑOZ Yo creo
que no lo sé.
DON DIEGO Pues decidme,
si es acaso forastero,
¿a qué a Sevilla ha venido
y dónde vive?, que quiero
ser su amigo.
MUÑOZ A tus preguntas
va de respuesta y de cuento:
mi señor es de Sevilla
natural y caballero,
pero caballero mozo,
con que te digo con esto
que tiene sus mocedades
y que es vasallo de Venus.[21]
Me parece que tres años
habrá, poco más o menos,
que, estando de cierta dama
una noche en el terrero,
por más señas que fue día
de San Clemente —no puedo
olvidarme, que no es fácil
olvidar que tuve miedo—
vio que de la misma reja
donde él sus finos requiebros
arrojaba, otro galán
tenía ocupado el puesto,
y así le fue necesario
tener al instante celos;
dellos armado, sacó
la espada, y con él riñendo
le[22] hirió muy mal, dejóle
porque le dejó por muerto,
y a Flandes, sin ver su dama,
tomó las de Villadiego.[23]

---

[21] "Venus" no destruye la asonancia e-o.

[22] Dialefa entre "le" e "hirió".

[23] *Tomar las de Villadiego*—"Phrase, que vale ausentarse impensadamente, ó hacer

DON DIEGO ([*Aparte*] ¡Raro caso! Mi enemigo
es don Juan, y ya por serlo
en el pecho se compiten
rencor y agradecimiento.)
¿Dónde le hallaré?

MUÑOZ No sé:
mas si no me engaño, creo
que es el que viene.

Sale DON JUAN.

DON JUAN Ir a casa
de Celestina deseo
a darla gracias del modo
con que con su agudo ingenio,
aunque a costa de Tacón,
me sacó de aquel empeño
de la casa de don Luis:
mas a mi enemigo veo;[24]
quiero, pues le encuentro aquí,
llegar.

DON DIEGO Si don Juan es, quiero
hablarle y a mis antiguas
quejas, con lo que le debo,
olvidar.

DON JUAN Hablaréle y
daré venganza a mis celos;
señor don Diego.

DON DIEGO Señor[25]
don Juan, deseaba veros,
y, aunque pudiera agraviado,
reconocido pretendo

---

fuga" (*Aut.*). Quizás haya un guiño por parte de sor Juana al considerar que Muñoz está hablando con don Diego.

[24] Supo del papel de don Diego en los vv. 1613–26.

[25] Para los vv. 2809–2835 de sor Juana, véanse vv. 3289–3300 del final de Vera.

sólo hablaros, que, entre dos
distantes varios afectos,
de agradecimiento y odio,
siempre pudo en nobles pechos
más que el odio vengativo
fiel el agradecimiento.

DON JUAN
Yo también, don Diego, os busco,
aunque con fin muy diverso;
pues un accidente acaso
me dijo que de mis celos
sois la causa, y de sus iras
hoy tomar venganza espero
en vos, y así vengativo
y no agradecido os quiero.
Yo os remito aquella deuda,
pues nada hice en defenderos,
que, estando vos solo, a mí
me debí solo el hacerlo;
y si entonces vuestra vida
defendí, fue previniendo
guardárosla por entonces
para quitárosla luego,
y así nada me debéis.

DON DIEGO
Pues que yo con lo que debo
he cumplido, y no admitís
que esté remiso mi acero,
por satisfacer en algo
el favor que hallé en el vuestro,
será preciso que riña.
Y pues aquéste no es puesto
donde puedan remitirse
las quejas a los aceros,
guïad adónde quisiereis,
que yo os seguiré.

DON JUAN
Supuesto
que estamos junto a Trïana,
irnos hacia allá podremos,
donde sin testigo pueda
concluirse nuestro empeño.

DON DIEGO
Vamos.

DON JUAN
Tú, Muñoz, te queda,

y en casa me aguarda. *Vanse.*

MUÑOZ Bueno,
a reñir van mano a mano,
si no me engaña mi ingenio,
pues en las señas que han dado,
alterados los acentos,
descompuestas las acciones
y arrugado el sobrecejo,
y irse los dos y dejarme;
sin duda el diablo anda suelto,
y ha de haber muertes de[26] hombres;
yo me voy luego al momento
a embarazar pesadumbres,
que soy buen cristiano viejo.

Al irse MUÑOZ, sale[n] DOÑA ANA y DOÑA BEATRIZ tapadas.

DOÑA ANA ¿Dijístele a Antonia dónde
íbamos?
DOÑA BEATRIZ Sí.
DOÑA ANA Mal has hecho;
pero Muñoz está allí.
Muñoz.
MUÑOZ ¿Quién?
DOÑA BEATRIZ Nosotras.
MUÑOZ Bueno.
Cuando yo juzgué que estabais
en la casa y aposento
ya de Celestina . . .
CELESTINA ¿Quién *Sale.*
me nombra?, cuando yo pienso
que más retirada estoy
del mundo y sólo me acuerdo
del regalo[27] de mi[28] alma,
porque el alma es lo primero.

---

[26] Dialefa entre "de" y "hombres".

[27] *Regalo*—"Se aplica assimismo à la comida y bebida delicada y exquisita". "Vale assimismo conveniencia, comodidad ù descanso, que se procura en orden à la persóna". (*Aut.*)

[28] Dialefa entre "mi" y "alma".

Aunque, bendito sea[29] Dios,
no lo hago mal con mi cuerpo.
¿Quién, pues, profana mi nombre
con su boca?

MUÑOZ A lindo tiempo
has llegado, Celestina,
que las damas que estás viendo
doña Beatriz y doña Ana
son.

CELESTINA ¡Cielos, qué es lo que veo!
Cuando a vuestra casa[30] iba
a dar cuenta por extenso
de todo lo que ha pasado
con el viejo sempiterno*, eterno
a pesar de mi retiro,
¡disfrazadas os encuentro!
¿Qué novedad es aquésta?

DOÑA ANA A hablarte en lo que hay de nuevo
mi prima y yo dispusimos
ir a tu cuarto, pues creo
que hay novedad.

CELESTINA Y muy grande.

MUÑOZ Señoras, al mayor riesgo
acudamos.

DOÑA BEATRIZ ¿Y cuál es?

MUÑOZ El que don Juan y don Diego
por ahí van desafiados
a Trïana, que, sabiendo
don Diego que era don Juan
su enemigo, ([*Aparte*] callar quiero
que fui yo quien se lo dijo,
por si importare a mi miedo)
le fue a buscar, y encontróle,
de que resultó que luego
se desafiaron, con que
es forzoso que el remedio
se busque.

---

[29] Sinéresis en "sea".
[30] Dialefa entre "casa" e "iba".

DOÑA ANA ¿Habrá más rigores?
¿Amor, hay más sentimientos?
Pues cuando a remediar iba
un peligro, quiere el cielo
que me mate otro mayor.
DOÑA BEATRIZ ¿No me bastaban mis celos,
don Diego, sino también
añadir al sentimiento
tanta copia de pesares
que asaltan mi amante pecho?
CELESTINA Señoras, dejaos[31] ahora
de referir vuestros duelos,
y a lo que importa acudamos.
DOÑA ANA Tú nos has de sacar de esto,
Celestina.
CELESTINA ¿Yo, señora?
Pero ya ha hallado mi ingenio
medio para salir bien;
¿queréis más que os dé un remedio
para estorbar la pendencia
y que no se maten?
DOÑA BEATRIZ Eso
pagará nuestra fineza
con el agradecimiento.
CELESTINA Pues lo que hablaros quería,
después contároslo puedo,
y en lo que se debe hacer
no se debe perder tiempo.
Es menester que al instante
—pues la prevención ha[32] hecho,
o la dicha, que vengáis
con disfraz, y según creo
han de estar cerca de aquí—
los busquéis, y con el medio
que os pareciere estorbéis
su pendencia, que yo quiero,
pues también está mi casa

[31] Sinéresis en "dejaos".
[32] Dialefa entre "ha" y "hecho".

tan cerca, ir allá al momento
a disponer ciertas cosas
para que cese su duelo.
Tú, Muñoz, vente conmigo.

DOÑA ANA Siempre juzgué hallar consuelo
en ti.

DOÑA BEATRIZ También de mi parte,
como es justo, lo agradezco;
vamos, doña Ana.

DOÑA ANA Beatriz,
vamos, no se pierda tiempo.

DOÑA BEATRIZ Adiós, Celestina.

CELESTINA Adiós.

DOÑA ANA Que luego a tu casa iremos. *Va[nse].*

CELESTINA ([*Aparte*] De esta suerte he conseguido
que me regalen por esto,
siendo ellas quien lo estorban.
Aprendan de mí los cuerdos
que miento, y nada me cuesta,
y me pagan lo que miento.) *Vanse.*

CUADRO IV

Sale[n] DON JUAN y DON DIEGO.

DON JUAN No pasemos adelante, [*romances*]
don Diego, que aqueste sitio,
aunque a Sevilla cercano,
retirado es del bullicio
de la gente, y ya mis iras
se corren de haber tenido
tres años, en que no supe
de vos, mi enojo remiso.

DON DIEGO Pues, don Juan, lo que la lengua
ha de decir, vengativo
lo diga el acero; bien *Riñen.*
se defiende.

DON JUAN — Más me irrita[33]
con su valor mi coraje.
DON DIEGO — Bien reñis.
DON JUAN — Riñen conmigo
mis celos.
DON DIEGO — ¿Que ya no acabe?

Prosiguen en reñir, y salen DOÑA ANA y DOÑA BEATRIZ tapadas.

DOÑA BEATRIZ — Dicha ha sido descubrirlos.
DOÑA ANA — Todo sucedía bien,
si mi padre en el camino
no nos hubiera encontrado.

Llégase DOÑA ANA a DON JUAN, y DOÑA BEATRIZ a DON DIEGO.

DOÑA BEATRIZ — Así hemos de dividirlos.
Caballero.
DOÑA ANA — Caballero.
DOÑA BEATRIZ — Que ya el serlo, vuestro brío
me lo ha dicho.
DOÑA ANA — Que ya el serlo,
vuestro gran valor me ha dicho.
DOÑA BEATRIZ — A una mujer socorred,
que las iras de un marido
y de un honor viene huyendo.
DOÑA ANA — Volved los valientes filos
a amparar una mujer,
que de un hermano ofendido
huyendo viene.[34]
DON DIEGO — ¿Cómo?[35]
DON JUAN — Pues, ¿cómo, si a mi enemigo
tengo en campaña?
DOÑA BEATRIZ — Dejad
eso ahora, pues ha sido

---

[33] "Irrita" destruye la asonancia i-o.

[34] Esta acción trae a la memoria el comienzo del argumento de *La dama duende* de Calderón, en el cual doña Angela le pide ayuda a don Manuel al huir, también tapada, de su hermano.

[35] Es un verso heptasilábico, a menos que se pronuncie "viene" como trisílabo.

evitar una desdicha,
en el que noble ha nacido,
la primera obligación.

DOÑA ANA Siempre es duelo más preciso
favorecer a una dama.

DON DIEGO Decís bien.

DON JUAN Bien habéis dicho.
Don Diego . . .

DON DIEGO Don Juan, a mí
me importa . . .

DON JUAN Yo necesito . . .

LOS DOS . . . ir sirviendo aquesta dama.

DON DIEGO Según esto, a un tiempo mismo
nos suspende igual empeño.

DON JUAN Es verdad, pero imagino
que el mío es inexcusable.

DON DIEGO También, don Juan, lo es el mío;
y así, pues que nuestro duelo
podemos después concluirlo.
Señoras, ya a vuestra[36] orden
estamos los dos.

DON JUAN Decidnos,
¿qué hemos de hacer?

DOÑA BEATRIZ Vos, seguidme.

DOÑA ANA Venid vos. ([*Aparte*] No determino
dónde llevarle.)

DOÑA BEATRIZ ([*Aparte*] No sé
dónde vaya, mas mi tío . . .)
Prima, tu padre.

Llégase DOÑA BEATRIZ a DOÑA ANA.

DOÑA ANA ¿Qué dices?
Sin duda nos ha seguido,
él nos conoció.

DOÑA BEATRIZ Eso es cierto,
porque, al encontrarnos, hizo
gran reparo.

[36] Dialefa entre "vuestra" y "orden".

DON JUAN ¿No venís?
DON DIEGO ¿Qué os detiene?
DOÑA ANA Aquí preciso
es hacer esto.
DOÑA BEATRIZ Yo quiero

Llégа[n]se DOÑA ANA a DON JUAN y DOÑA BEATRIZ a DON DIEGO, y se les descubren.

descubrirme y prevenirlo
a don Diego: yo, don Diego,
soy.
DON DIEGO ¿Pues vos en este sitio?
DOÑA BEATRIZ Sí, oídme.
DOÑA ANA Don Juan, doña Ana
soy.
DON JUAN ¡Ah, ingrata, qué has venido
al peligro de don Diego!
DOÑA ANA Sólo vine a tu peligro,
don Juan, aunque ya parece
que antes he llegado al mío;
porque mi padre me sigue,
que le detengas te pido.
DOÑA BEATRIZ Deténle por Dios.
DON JUAN Segura
vé.
DON DIEGO Vé segura.
DOÑA ANA El arbitrio,[37]
mal haya de los disfraces;
vamos prima.
DOÑA BEATRIZ Ya te sigo.

Vanse las dos, y sale DON LUIS al paño.

DON LUIS En cada cosa que encuentro
toma más cuerpo el delito

[37] *Arbitrio*—"El médio que se propóne extraordinário, y no regular para conseguir algun fin" (*Aut.*).

de mi[38] hija, pues en casa
no la he[39] hallado, y me dijo
Antonia, aunque amenazada
por mí, que había salido
disfrazada, con su prima,
y que son las dos colijo
que por aquí fueron, pero

Va saliendo, y al salir ve a DON DIEGO, y se detiene.

hacia allí a don Diego miro,
a quien ofendido busco.
¿Qué haré? ¡Ah honor!

DON DIEGO Que era tío
de doña Beatriz don Luis
nunca supe.

DON JUAN ([*Aparte*] ¿Quién se ha visto
obligado a hacer espaldas
a sus celos?)

DON LUIS Si averiguo
que la tapada es mi[40] hija,
ya mis recelos confirmo
con evidencia, y así
seguirla esta vez elijo,
que después veré a don Diego.

DON DIEGO Señor don Luis, yo os suplico
os detengáis. *Detiénenle.*

DON LUIS Perdonadme,
que no puedo.

DON JUAN Que deciros
tenemos don Diego y yo,
y es preciso.

DON LUIS Más preciso
es el motivo que llevo.

DON DIEGO Sólo un instante os pedimos
nos oigas.

---

[38] Dialefa entre "mi" e "hija".
[39] Dialefa entre "he" y "hallado".
[40] Dialefa entre "mi" e "hija".

DON LUIS Haréis que os diga
que unas mujeres que sigo
temo perderlas; ¿queréis
más? Ya con esto os he dicho
mi prisa y la causa de ella.

DON DIEGO ¿Pues vuestra edad, vuestro juicio,
don Luis, anda en tales pasos?

DON LUIS No son mis canas indicios
de sospecha: ea, dejadme
por Dios.

DON DIEGO ([*Aparte*] ¿Si habrán ya salido
donde estén seguras?)

DON LUIS Pero
ya advierto . . . ¡Ah dolor prolijo,
que con esta detención
de vista las he perdido!
Ya no es posible alcanzarlas.

DON JUAN Mas, señor don Luis, creímos
de veros . . .

DON LUIS ([*Aparte*] Ya no hay remedio.
Mas pues aquí mi enemigo
tengo, no se pierda todo.)
Supuesto que habéis querido
que me detenga, será
a reñir: sacad el limpio
acero, don Diego, que
estoy de vos ofendido.
Y pues don Juan se halla aquí,
será de entrambos padrino.

Sacan las espadas, y DON JUAN los detiene.

DON DIEGO Aunque no alcanzo la causa,
nunca en la campaña estilo* acostumbro
preguntarla.

DON LUIS Pues reñid.

DON JUAN Eso no, porque conmigo
tiene empezado don Diego
un duelo en aqueste sitio,
y ha de acabarle primero.

DON LUIS Es mi duelo más antiguo,

quizá, y más grave que el vuestro.

DON DIEGO Conformaos, pues, que mi brío
os sabrá satisfacer.

DON JUAN Es mi duelo más preciso,
que ése no será de amor,
y estotro sí, que ha nacido
por dos mujeres que ahora
de aqueste lugar se han ido.
([*Aparte*] Así a su razón respondo,
y consigo, de camino,
deslumbrarle la sospecha
con que a doña Ana ha seguido,
que no ha de creer que estaba
con los dos.)

DON LUIS ([*Aparte*] ¡Cielos, qué he oído!
Por mi hija riñen sin duda,
y ya me ofrece el destino
otro enemigo en don Juan:
yo estoy ciego.) También mío
es ese duelo, y así
reñidle, don Juan, conmigo.

Riñe con DON JUAN y DON DIEGO lo estorba.

DON DIEGO No puede ser, que primero
fui yo de vos elegido,
y he de reñir yo o ninguno.

DON JUAN Yo también digo lo mismo.

DON LUIS ([*Aparte*] ¿Qué haré, honor, que ya mi agravio,
en dos partes dividido,
más que se acaba se aumenta?
Ya mejor hubiera sido
hablar a don Diego en paz
y a solas, sin dar indicios
tan públicos de mi ofensa;[41]
yo lo erré, el dolor impío
me precipitó, mas, pues
me da bastante motivo

[41] Véase la nota al v. 2622 de SJ, y también la al v. 3520 de VT.

el embarazo del duelo,
enmendarlo así imagino.)
DON JUAN ¿Qué resolvéis?
DON DIEGO ¿Qué decís?
DON LUIS Que pues se halla tan ambiguo
el modo de nuestro duelo,
yo por ahora desisto
dél, como tampoco[42]
le prosigáis.
DON JUAN Yo el partido
acepto. ([*Aparte*] Así lograré
saber luego dónde ha ido
doña Ana.)
DON DIEGO Pues yo también.
([*Aparte*] Que deste modo consigo
saber luego dónde fue
Beatriz.)
DON LUIS Pues ya suspendidos
quedan nuestros sentimientos,
yo os buscaré.
DON DIEGO Yo lo mismo
haré.
DON JUAN Yo también. Adiós.
DON LUIS Adiós. ([*Aparte*] ¡Ah crüel martirio[43]
del honor! Voy a apurar
los enojos que reprimo.) *Vase.*
DON JUAN ([*Aparte*] Iré a ver a Celestina,
que, como está cerca, asilo
quizás será de doña Ana.) *Vase.*
DON DIEGO ([*Aparte*] Ir a casa determino
de Celestina, y por que* para que
pueda entrar desconocido,
iré por la puerta falsa,
quizá con este motivo
sabré alguna cosa y daré[44]
a mis males el alivio.) *Vanse.*

---

[42] Este verso es un hexasílabo.
[43] Añado "Adiós" para constar el octosílabo
[44] Es eneasílabo este verso.

CUADRO V

Sale[n] DOÑA ANA, [DOÑA] BEATRIZ y CELESTINA.

DOÑA ANA Esto ha pasado, y a ir[45]
a casa no me he atrevido,
hasta saber si mi padre
sin recelo está.
DOÑA BEATRIZ Preciso
es nuestro riesgo, porque él,
prima, nos ha conocido
sin duda.
CELESTINA ([*Aparte*] ¡Lástima[46] es
cuál están los angelitos!)
DOÑA ANA Celestina, si tu ciencia
a las dos deste conflicto
no nos sacas, nuestra vida
hoy corre grande peligro.
CELESTINA El lance es dificultoso.
([*Aparte*] Mis embustes imagino
que no bastan para[47] esto.)
DOÑA BEATRIZ De ti espero.
DOÑA ANA De ti fío.
CELESTINA Señoras, vamos al caso,
que el caso es un poco vivo:
tú estás de don Juan celosa,
tú de don Diego lo mismo,
don Juan lo está de don Diego.
DOÑA BEATRIZ Nunca yo hubiera atendido
a sus ruegos.
DOÑA ANA Nunca oyera
yo sus amantes suspiros.
CELESTINA Y estando los dos riñendo,
lograsteis el dividirlos,
y entonces llegó tu padre.

---

45 Hay dos dialefas en este verso.
46 Dialefa entre "Lástima" y "es".
47 Dialefa entre "pero" y "esto".

DOÑA BEATRIZ Y lo que hemos referido
pasó.
CELESTINA A que se añade que,
como también os he dicho,
está con grandes recelos
de don Diego, y que a eso vino
a mi casa.
DOÑA ANA ¡Yo estoy muerta!
CELESTINA No hallo remedio en mis libros
para deslumbrar recelos
de un padre; si de un marido
fueran.
DOÑA BEATRIZ Por Dios, Celestina,
no nos dejes.
CELESTINA Ya un arbitrio
se me ofrece.

Sale[n] LA JUSTICIA y TACON, y LAS DAMAS se tapan.

[ALGUACIL] 1 La justicia.
TACON ¿Si para esto habrá otro hechizo?
DOÑA BEATRIZ ([*Aparte*] ¡Ay mujer más infeliz!)
DOÑA ANA ([*Aparte*] ¡Ay más infeliz destino!
También esto me sucede
mal, pues lugar no he tenido
de avisar a Celestina
deste caso.)
CELESTINA ¡Dios bendito!
¡Justicia en mi casa! ¿Cómo
es esto?
[ALGUACIL] 2 ¿Cuál es, decidnos,
Celestina?
TACON Aquélla[48] es.
CELESTINA ¡Cielos! ¿Quién en tal conflito
me podrá socorrer?
TACON Mira
si hay otro viejo escondido
que te ayude.

[48] Dialefa entre "Aquella" y "es".

Sale DON LUIS.

DON LUIS A Celestina,
pues ya lo sabe, he querido
ver . . . Mas gente hay aquí, voyme.
CELESTINA ¡A qué buen tiempo ha venido
hoy don Luis! Señor don Luis,
amparadme.
DON LUIS Ya me han visto
y no puedo irme.
DOÑA ANA ([*Aparte*] ¿Qué es esto?
Mi padre es.)
DOÑA BEATRIZ ([*Aparte*] ¡Cielos, mi tío!)
TACON ¡Que esta borracha hechicera
tenga en la manga metido
siempre a este viejo fantasma!
DOÑA BEATRIZ ¡De temor aun no respiro!

Sale DON JUAN.

DON JUAN De aquesta suerte sabré . . .

Sale DON DIEGO.

DON DIEGO De aquesta suerte consigo
el saber . . . ([*Aparte*] ¡Pero don Juan!)
DON JUAN ([*Aparte*] ¡Mas allí a don Diego he visto!)
DON LUIS ([*Aparte*] ¡Don Diego y don Juan aquí!)
TACON ¿Quién, diablos, habrá traído
a mi amo y a estos hombres?[49]
DOÑA ANA ([*Aparte*] ¡Don Juan!)
DOÑA BEATRIZ ([*Aparte*] ¡Don Diego, qué miro!)
DOÑA ANA ([*Aparte*] Ya podrá tener con esto
nuestra pena algún alivio.)
[ALGUACIL] 1 Daos[50] a prisión, Celestina.
CELESTINA Señores, ¿qué he cometido
para prenderme?

---

[49] Hay dos dialefas en este verso.
[50] Sinéresis en "Daos".

[ALGUACIL] 2 En la cárcel
se dirá vuestro delito.
TACON Señor, agárrela usted, *A la JUSTICIA.*
porque, si no, yo imagino
que se pondrá en Trapisonda,[51]
si se le antoja, de un brinco.
CELESTINA ([*Aparte*] Aquí yacen mis enredos
que tanto los he querido.)
Mi señor don Luis, valedme.
DON LUIS Caballero, aunque es preciso *A la JUSTICIA.*
obdecer la justicia,
y más yo, pues he nacido
con aquesa obligación,
os ruego que compasivo
por ahora suspendáis
vuestro rigor.
[ALGUACIL] 1 Nuestro oficio
obliga a no obedeceros;
ea, agarradla.
CELESTINA Pasito.
[ALGUACIL] 2 Y por si cómplices son
esas damas, es preciso
reconocerlas.

Quieren reconocer las DAMAS.

DON JUAN Primero
desta espada por el filo
habéis de pasar, si acaso
proseguís.
DON DIEGO Y yo lo mismo
tengo de hacer, pues primero
morir en la empresa elijo.
DON LUIS ([*Aparte*] Mucho el corazón recelo:
¡a espacio, honor!)
DOÑA ANA El peligro,

---

[51] *Trapisonda*—"Bulla, ò riña con voces, ò acciones" (*Autoridades*).

Decúbrense a los DOS.

si me conoce mi padre,
es cierto.

DOÑA BEATRIZ Si mi tío
me conoce, es grande el riesgo.

DON JUAN De que tú hayas presumido *A DOÑA ANA.*
eso, mi valor se corre.

DON DIEGO Poco fías de mis bríos. *A DOÑA BEATRIZ.*

[ALGUACIL] 1 Esto ha de ser, perdonad,
señoras.

LOS DOS Ya os hemos dicho
que es en vano la porfía.

Sale ANTONIA tapada, y se descubre.

ANTONIA Señoras, mi amo . . . ¡qué miro!
([*Aparte*] Válgame Santa Susana,[52]
a quien tanto han perseguido
los viejos, que aqueste viejo
me ha cogido en el garlito*.) trampa

DON LUIS Ya me ha dicho que son ellas
esta causa; así imagino

Saca la daga y DON DIEGO la defiende,
y DOÑA BEATRIZ se descubre.

vengarme, traidora[53] hija:
este acero vengativo . . .

DOÑA BEATRIZ Tente, señor, que no soy.

DON DIEGO Detened, don Luis, los filos.

DON LUIS ([*Aparte*] ¿Qué es aquesto? Cuando pienso
que don Diego amante fino
es de mi hija, a Beatriz[54]
junto a su lado la he visto.

[52] Alusión bíblica a Susana, la que fue perseguida por dos viejos nada honestos.
[53] Dialefa entre "traidora" e "hija".
[54] Dialefa entre "mi" e "hija" y sinéresis de "Beatriz".

Mas con mi enojo otro examen
nuevamente determino.)

Va a dar a DOÑA ANA [y] DON JUAN la defiende.

DOÑA ANA Detente, señor, espera.
DON JUAN No podrás, pues solicito
primero morir.
DON LUIS ¿Qué es esto?
([*Aparte*] ¿Qué confusiones, qué abismos
son éstos que por mí pasan,
a ser de mi honor cuchillo?)
Mujer, ¿qué encantos son éstos? *A CELESTINA.*
¿Tú no me diste el aviso
de que don Diego era quien
en mi jardín había[55] visto?
CELESTINA Es verdad.
DON LUIS Pues ¿cómo ahora
de don Juan me hallo ofendido?
CELESTINA Si te reportas y atiendes,
tendrá tu honor el alivio
que desea, y yo quizá
saldré de aqueste peligro
en que estoy.
DOÑA ANA ¿A qué veniste,
mujer?
ANTONIA Sólo a preveniros
que mi[56] amo os echó menos
en casa y andaba listo
buscándoos.[57] ([*Aparte*] Gracias al chisme
que reveló tamañito
mi miedo.)
DON LUIS Por ver si puede
encontrar el pesar mío
algún desengaño, que
del confuso laberinto

[55] Sinéresis en "había".
[56] Dialefa entre "mi" y "amo".
[57] Sinéresis de "buscándoos".

me saque, escucharte quiero.
([*Aparte*] ¡Ah indigno crüel estilo
del honor, pues no repara,
por salir de su peligro,
el medio indigno, si[58] es
desengaño el medio indigno!)

[ALGUACIL] 1 Nosotros, por ver si puede
tu habilidad dar indicios
de tu disculpa, te damos
licencia.

CELESTINA Pues el oído
prevenid, por que* sin duda — para que
quedéis todos.

TODOS Ya te oímos.

DOÑA ANA ([*Aparte*] ¡Ay Dios, si dirá mi amor!
Pero ya en vano me aflijo,
pues hoy tantos accidentes
bastantemente le han dicho.)

CELESTINA Pues sabed que yo en mi vida — [*redondillas*]
no aprendí ciencia ninguna,
porque mi buena fortuna
ha estribado en ser creída.
Soplándome el aire grato,
con mi maña di en mentir;
con el plato del fingir,
me dio al mediodía el plato.[59]
Con lo que a unos oía,
a[60] otros respuesta daba,
y así con estos ganaba
crédito mi astrología.

TACON Pues saber, como sé yo,
que el día de San Clemente
a don Diego hirió impaciente
mi amo, ¿no fue ciencia?

CELESTINA No,

---

[58] Dialefa entre "si" y "es".

[59] *Poner el plato*—"Phrase que vale poner á uno en ocasion de hacer ù decir lo que no pensára" (*Aut.*). También hay juego de palabras o antanaclasis en vv. 3343–44 que explica el modo de ganarse la vida.

[60] Dialefa entre "a" y "otros".

que, cuando tu amo llegaba,
doña Ana a preguntar vino
si don Juan estaba fino
y si en la ausencia la amaba;
por poderlo adivinar,
me dijo hora, nombre y día,
con que en esta astrología
poco tuve que estudiar;
¿no es verdad esto, señora? *A DOÑA ANA.*

DOÑA ANA Sí, que negarlo no puedo.

TACON Vaya, yo te lo concedo:
mas dime, embelecadora
vieja, ¿tú no adivinaste
que mi amo a España venía,
y le trajiste aquel día,
a un conjuro que ordenaste,
a ver a doña Ana?, que
Antonia me lo contó;
di, pues, ahora, ¿qué esto no
fue hechizo?

CELESTINA Pues no lo fue,
porque don Juan deseó
ver a Beatriz, que, al entrar
en Sevilla, vio cazar,
y a mi casa se llegó
a hablarme en ello, y así
supe que en Sevilla estaba,
y también que le importaba
ir a su casa advertí
a unas cartas que traía
de Flandes.

DON JUAN Eso así[61] es,
por más señas que después
de las cartas.

TACON Y ese día
mismo fue el día fatal
en que esta vieja embustera

---

[61] Dialefa entre "así" y "es".

hizo creer que yo[62] era
ladrón, con una infernal
astucia.

DON JUAN Pues, Celestina,
según eso, ¿tú no fuiste
aquélla que dispusiste
con tu maña peregrina
que yo a doña Beatriz viese
en cas* de doña Ana? casa

CELESTINA No,
que con ella se hospedó,
y fue preciso estuviese
allí.

DOÑA BEATRIZ ([*Aparte*] ¡Pluguieran[63] los cielos
no fuera tanta verdad,
pues así mi voluntad
no hubiera hallado unos celos!)

DON LUIS Y la ilusión que pasó
por el cristalino espejo,
que yo admiré en su reflejo,
¿no fue hechicería?

CELESTINA No.

DON DIEGO Y el salir sin ser sentido
del aposento en que estaba,
cuando don Luis lo miraba
por el espejo, ¿no ha sido
encanto?

CELESTINA No.

LOS DOS. Pues, ¿qué fue?

CELESTINA Mandarme tú que supiera
el que te agravió quién era;
confusa me hallé, por que
no supe qué medio dar.
A este tiempo, la salida
doña Beatriz afligida
me mandó solicitar

---

[62] Dialefa entre "yo" y "era".

[63] *Pluguieran*—Viene de verbo placer. "Ojalá que los cielos se hubieran complacido de que . . . ."

de don Diego, y con acierto
del espejo me valí.

ANTONIA
Sí yo a don Diego le di
la entrada por verle muerto
de amor, aunque despreciado
fue de mi ama, que a su amor
siempre trató con rigor.

DON JUAN
([*Aparte*] Ya sosiega mi cuidado
y mi enamorada vida
alienta, ya sin recelos,
pues la tormenta de celos
veo ya desvanecida.)

DON DIEGO
([*Aparte*] Pues me engañó Antonia, ya
de mi Beatriz los enojos
satisfaré, que a sus ojos
adorando el alma está.)

TACON
Ven acá, vieja trapillo,
dime, ¿no fue encantamiento
cuando, en tu mismo aposento,
para quitarme el bolsillo
hiciste mágicamente
a algún demonio alquilón
que trajese al señor don
Luis, que se halla aquí presente?

CELESTINA
No fue encanto, porque, estando
en mi casa cuando entraste
y robarme procuraste,
estaba con él hablando;
veniste, y a un aposento
por no ser visto se fue;
con que fue fácil el que
pareciese encantamiento.

DON LUIS
Verdad es cuanto has contado.

[ALGUACIL] 1
Pues vámonos, si es así,
que ya no hay qué hacer aquí.

CELESTINA
Teneos,[64] que aun no está aclarado
todo, y en esta ocasión
nada oculto ha de quedar.

[64] Sinéresis en "Teneos".

([*Aparte*] Así me pienso vengar,
señores, deste bribón.)
Palabra me tiene dada
de casamiento, y, por no
quererla cumplir, fingió
todo esto y tal campanada
ha dado.

TACON ¡Ay tan gran maldad!

CELESTINA Ponedle en la cárcel luego.

TACON ¡Jesús, qué embuste! Reniego
de mí mismo.

[ALGUACIL] 2 Si es verdad,
casaos[65] luego, o desde aquí
iréis a la cárcel preso.

TACON Sólo me faltaba[66] eso:
bruja, ¿qué quieres de mí?
¿Qué no[67] hay quien te acogote?

[ALGUACIL] 1 Vamos.

TACON Don Juan, mi señor . . .

CELESTINA Pues si no quiere ir, mejor
será que en algo me dote.

TACON Yo dotarte, ¿qué he escuchado?
A echarme por un balcón
voy.

[ALGUACIL] 2 Venid sin dilación.

DON JUAN Dejadle ahora, y pues ha dado
Celestina claridad
a todas nuestras sospechas,
y miramos ya deshechas
las dudas con la verdad,
ya es tiempo . . .

DON LUIS Tened, y reparo[68]
haced que, aunque de ese modo
ya se haya aclarado todo,
mi honor no ha quedado claro.

---

[65] Sinéresis en "casaos".

[66] Dialefa entre "faltaba" y "eso".

[67] Dialefa entre "no" y "hay".

[68] Es eneasílabo este verso.

Y pues a mi honor los dos
igual ofensa habéis hecho
sin dejarme satisfecho,
no os habéis de ir, vive Dios.

DON JUAN En satisfaceros gano,
pues fue mi sospecha vana;
ésta es mi mano, doña Ana.

DOÑA ANA Esta, don Juan, es mi mano.

DON DIEGO Y por que* duda ninguna — para que
le quede a vuestro cuidado,
con Beatriz estoy casado.

DOÑA BEATRIZ Feliz es ya mi fortuna.

DON LUIS Y la mía, pues consigo
ver ya mi honor sin recelo
y acabado nuestro duelo.

DON JUAN Y también el nuestro.

MUÑOZ Digo,
Antonia, esa mano venga,
puesto que cualquier lacayo
puede casarse al soslayo
sin que nada se prevenga.

ANTONIA Norabuena, aunque has callado
y nunca lugar ha habido
de agenciar el ser marido
y haberme galanteado,
toma esta mano divina,
que es envidia del hollín*, — negro de humo
y aquí, señores, da fin
La segunda Celestina.[69]

FIN.

[69] Además de las razones aducidas en la introducción sobre el título de la comedia, ¿es posible que sor Juana llamara a su conclusión la "segunda" sobre la Celestina salazariana? Tampoco se encuentra alusión alguna a un contexto real o cortesano en esta versión sorjuanina.

Bibliografia[1]

Alonso, Dámaso y Carlos Bousoño. *Seis calas en la expresión literaria española.* 2a edición. Madrid: Gredos, 1956.

Anónimo. *Carta en que, con ocasión de haber aprobado el Padre Guerra, de la Santísima Trinidad, las comedias del tiempo presente en la 5 Parte de Calderón, dice los inconvenientes que hay en su representación* (1682). Véase Vitse, págs 146–62.

Bances Candamo, Francisco de. *Teatro de los teatros* (1690). Véase Cotarelo, núm 26, págs. 73–82.

Barrera y Leirado, Cayetano Alberto de la. *Catálogo bibliográfico y biográfico del teatro antiguo español, desde sus orígenes hasta medianos del siglo XVIII.* Madrid, 1860.

Buck, Donald C. "Juan Salvo y Vela and the Rise of the *Comedia de Magia*: The Magician as Anti-Hero." *Hispania* 69.2 (1986): 251–61.

Caldera, Ermanno. "La magia negada. *El hechizo sin hechizo* de Salazar y Torres." *Diálogos hispánicos de Amsterdam* 8.2 (1989): 311–22.

Calderón de la Barca, Pedro. "Aprobación." En la *Cítara de Apolo* (1681).

———. *Cuarta parte de comedias nuevas de don Pedro Calderón de la Barca.* Madrid: Joseph Fernández de Buendía, 1672.

———. *La dama duende.* Ed. A. Valbuena Briones. Madrid: Cátedra, 1987.

———. *Dramas.* Vol. 1 de *Obras completas.* Ed. A. Valbuena Briones. Madrid: Aguilar, 1969.

———. *El médico de su honra.* Vol. 2 de *Dramas de honor.* Ed. A. Valbuena Briones. Madrid: Espasa-Calpe, 1965.

———. *Novena parte de comedias.* Ed. Juan de Vera Tassis y Villarroel. Madrid: Francisco Sanz, 1691 and 1694.

———. *Verdadera quinta parte de comedias.* Ed. Juan de Vera Tassis y Villarroel. Madrid: Francisco Sanz, 1682.

[1] La fecha en paréntesis que aparece después de las obras citadas en Cotarelo y Vitse representa el año de su composición, cuando éste se sabe, y no necesariamente el de su publicación.

Caramuel de Lobkowitz, Juan. *Epístola XXI* (1668). Véase Vitse.

Caro Baroja, Julio. *Teatro popular y magia*. Madrid: Revista de Occidente, 1974.

Castro, Adolfo de, ed. *Poetas líricos de los siglos XVI y XVII*, II. Vol. 42 de la *Biblioteca de Autores Españoles*. Madrid, 1857.

Clavijo y Fajardo, José de. *El pensador matritense* (1763). Véase Cotarelo, núm 57, págs. 151–60.

Consejo Real de Castilla. *Consulta* (1648). Véase Cotarelo, núm. 61, págs. 165–69.

Cotarelo y Mori, Emilio. *Bibliografía de las controversias sobre la licitud del teatro en España*. Madrid: Est. Tip. de la "Rev. de Archivos, Bibl. y Museos," 1904.

Crocetti, María Martino. "*La dama duende*: Spatial and Hymeneal Dialectics." En *The Perception of Women in Spanish Theater of the Golden Age*, ed. Anita K. Stoll y Dawn L. Smith, 51–66. Lewisburg, Pa.: Bucknell Univ. Press, 1991.

Cruickshank, Don W. "Don Juan de Vera Tassis y Villarroel." *Aureum Saeculum Hispanum. Beitrage zu texten des Siglo de Oro. Festschrift für Hans Flasche zum 70. Geburtstag*. Wiesbaden: Franz Steiner, 1983, pp. 43–57.

Cruz, Fray Jerónimo de la. *Job evangélico* (1635). Véase Cotarelo, núm. 71, págs. 202–4.

Cruz, Sor Juana Inés de la, y Agustín de Salazar y Torres. *La segunda Celestina*. Ed. Guillermo Schmidhuber, con la colaboración de Olga Martha Peña Doria. México, D.F.: Vuelta, 1990.

Diccionario de Autoridades. Madrid: Real Academia Española, 1726–39. Ed. facs. Madrid: Gredos, 1969.

Diccionario de la lengua española. 2 vol. Madrid: Real Academia Española, 1984.

Enciclopedia Espasa-Calpe.

Fomperosa y Quintana, P. Pedro. *El buen celo* (1682) y *Eutrapelia* (1683). Véase Cotarelo, núm. 92, págs. 262–69.

Foucault, Michel. *The History of Sexuality. Volume I: An Introduction*. Trans. Robert Hurley. New York: Vintage Books, 1990.

———. *The Order of Things*. New York: Vintage Books, 1973.

———. "What Is Enlightenment?" En *The Foucault Reader*, ed. Paul Rabinow, 32–50. New York: Pantheon Books, 1984.

García Berrio, Antonio. *Intolerancia de poder y protesta popular en el Siglo de Oro: Los debates sobre la licitud moral del teatro*. Málaga: Universidad de Málaga, 1978.

Gili y Gaya, Samuel. *Curso superior de sintaxis española*. Barcelona: Biblograf, 1964.

Guerra y Ribera, Fray Manuel de. "Aprobación." En la *Verdadera quinta parte de comedias de don Pedro Calderón de la Barca* (1682). Véase Cotarelo, núm. 102, págs. 329–41.

Gutiérrez de los Ríos, Francisco. *El hombre práctico, o discursos sobre su conocimiento y enseñanzas* (1680). Véase Vitse, págs. 130–46.

Hermenegildo, Alfredo. "Los signos condicionantes de la representación: El bloque didascálico." En *Critical Essays on the Literatures of Spain and Spanish America*, ed. Luis T. González-del-Valle and Julio Baena, 121–36. Boulder: Society of Spanish and Spanish-American Studies, 1991.

Herrera, P. Agustín de (alias don Antonio Puente Hurtado). *Discurso teológico y político sobre la Aprobación del P. Guerra* (1682). Véase Cotarelo, núm. 108, págs. 353–60.

Herrero García, Miguel. *Ideas de los españoles del siglo XVII*. Madrid: Gredos, 1966.

Hildner, David J. "Secuencias calderonianas de capa y espada: ¿'Sucesos caseros'?" *Bulletin of the Comediantes* 45.1 (1993): 67–75.

Honig, Edwin. "Flickers of Incest on the Face of Honor: Calderón's *Phantom Lady*." *Tulane Drama Review* 6 (1962): 69–105.

Jesús María, Fray José de. *Excelencias de la castidad* (1600). Véase Cotarelo, núm. 115, págs. 367–84.

Jovellanos, Gaspar M. de. *Memoria sobre los espectáculos* (1790). Véase Cotarelo, núm. 117, págs. 384–87.

Junta Superior. *Dictamen sobre lo ilícito de las comedias* (1672). Véase Cotarelo, núm. 118, págs. 387–90.

Lara, Gaspar Agustín de. *Obelisco fúnebre, pirámide funesto que construía, a la inmortal memoria de D. Pedro Calderón de la Calderón*. Madrid: Eugenio Rodríguez, 1684.

Larson, Catherine. "*La dama duende* and the Shifting Characterization of Calderón's Diabolical Angel." En *The Perception of Women in Spanish Theater of the Golden Age*, ed. Anita K. Stoll y Dawn L. Smith, 33–50. Lewisburg, Pa.: Bucknell Univ. Press, 1991.

Leal, Luis. "Una obra recuperada de Sor Juana." *Vuelta* 169 (1990): 44–45.

Leeming, David Adams. *The World of Myth*. New York: Oxford Univ. Press, 1990.

Machado de Chaves, Juan. *Confesor perfecto* (1640). Véase Cotarelo, núm. 128, págs. 419–20.

Maravall, José Antonio. *Teatro y literatura en la sociedad barroca*. Madrid: Seminarios y Ediciones, 1972.

Maria y Campos, Armando de. *Guía de representaciones teatrales en la Nueva*

España (siglos XVI al XVIII). México, D.F.: B. Costa-Amic, 1959.

Mariana, P. Juan de. *Tratado de los espectáculos* (1609). Véase Cotarelo, núm. 135, págs. 429–36.

Maura Gamazo, Gabriel. *Carlos II y su Corte*. 2 vol. Madrid, 1911–15.

Menéndez Pelayo, Marcelino. Vol. III de *Orígenes de la novela*. Buenos Aires, 1946.

Mesonero Romanos, Ramón de, ed. *Dramáticos posteriores a Lope de Vega*, II. Vol. 49 de *Biblioteca de Autores Españoles*. Madrid: Atlas, 1951.

Moraleda, Pilar. "La función del espejo en *El encanto es la hermosura* de Salazar y Torres." *Dianoia* (México D.F.) 3–4 (1989): 105–14. [No pude obtener este estudio por "Interlibrary Loan" en EE.UU.]

Mujica, Barbara. "Tragic Elements in Calderón's *La dama duende*." *Kentucky Romance Quarterly* 16 (1969): 303–28.

O'Connor, Thomas Austin. "A Bibliographical Note on Salazar y Torres' *Cytara de Apolo*." *Romance Notes* 15 (1973): 129–31.

———. "La desmitificación de Celestina en *El encanto es la hermosura* de Salazar y Torres." En *Actas del I Congreso Internacional sobre "La Celestina*." Madrid: Hispam, 1977, pp. 339–45.

———. "Don Agustín de Salazar y Torres: A Bibliography of Primary Sources." *Bulletin of Bibliography and Magazine Notes* 32, no. 4 (December 1975): 158–61; 167; 180.

———. "Los enredos de una pieza. El contexto histórico-teatral de *El encanto es la hermosura* o *La segunda Celestina* de Salazar y Torres, Vera Tassis y sor Juana." *Literatura Mexicana* 3.2 (1992): 283–303.

———. "La gramática y retórica del honor calderoniano: Las finezas como principio substancial." *Homenaje a Hans Flasche*, ed. Karl Hermann Körner y Günther Zimmermann 155–61. Stuttgart: Franz Steiner, 1991.

———. "*Infantas, Conformidad*, and Marriages of State: Observations on the *Loa* to Calderón's *La púrpura de la rosa*." *Bulletin of Hispanic Studies* 70 (1993): 175–85.

———. "The Knight of Olmedo and Oedipus: Perspectives on a Spanish Tragedy." *Hispanic Review* 48 (1980): 391–413.

———. "Language, Irony and Death: The Poetry of Salazar y Torres' *El encanto es la hermosura*." *Romanische Forschungen* 90 (1978): 60–69.

———. "A Lost Play of Salazar y Torres." *Bulletin of the Comediantes* 25 (1973): 40–43.

———. "On the Authorship of *El encanto es la hermosura*: A Curious Case of Dramatic Collaboration." *Bulletin of the Comediantes* 26 (1974): 31–34.

———. "On Dating the *Comedias* of Agustín de Salazar y Torres: A Provisional Study." *Hispanófila* 67 (1979): 73–81.

Parker, Alexander A. "The Spanish Drama of the Golden Age: A Method of Analysis and Interpretation". En *The Great Playwrights*, ed. Eric Bentley, 1:679–707. Garden City, NY: Doubleday, 1970.

Pascual Buxó, José. "Las vueltas de Sor Juana." *La Jornada Semanal* 76 (1990): 29–35 y *Nuevo Texto Crítico* 4.7 (1991): 197–204.

Paz, Octavio. "Azar o justicia." *Proceso* 710 (1990): 53.

———. *Sor Juana o las trampas de la fe*. México, D.F.: Fondo de Cultura Económica, 1985.

Ramos del Manzano, Francisco. *Com. ad Leg. Iul et Pap*. (1677). Véase Cotarelo, núm. 167, págs. 517–19.

Regueiro, José M. *Spanish Drama of the Golden Age. A Catalogue of the "Comedia" Collection in the University of Pennsylvania Libraries*. New Haven: Research Publications, 1971.

Sabat de Rivers, Georgina. "Los problemas de *La segunda Celestina*." *Nueva Revista de Filología Hispánica* 40 (1992): 493–512.

Salazar y Torres, Agustín de. *Cítara de Apolo*. 2 vol. Madrid: Francisco Sanz, 1681.

Shergold, N. D., and J. E. Varey. *Representaciones palaciegas: 1603–1699. Estudio y documentos*. Vol. 1 de *Fuentes para la historia del teatro en España*. London: Tamesis, 1982.

Smith, Barbara. "Section IV: Women, Myth and Ritual." En el Capítulo "Greece" de *The Feminist Companion to Mythology*, ed. Carolyne Larrington. London: Pandora Press, 1992.

ter Horst, Robert. "The Ruling Temper of Calderón's *La dama duende*." *Bulletin of the Comediantes* 27 (1975): 68–72.

Varey, John E. "*La dama duende*, de Calderón: Símbolos y escenografía." En *Calderón: Actas del 'Congreso Internacional sobre Calderón y el teatro español del Siglo de Oro'*. Madrid: Anejos de la revista "Segismundo," 6, 1983. I: 165–83.

Varey, J. E., and N. D. Shergold, con la colaboración de Charles Davis. *Comedias en Madrid: 1603–1709. Reportorio y estudio bibliográfico*. Vol. 9 de *Fuentes para la historia del teatro en España*. London: Tamesis, 1989.

Villarroel, Fray Gaspar de. *Gobierno eclesiástico* (1646). Véase Cotarelo, núm. 210, págs. 595–605.

Vitse, Marc. *Eléments pour une théorie de théâtre espagnol du XVIIe siècle*. Toulouse: France-Ibérie Recherche, Université de Toulouse-Le Mirail, 1988.

Wardropper, Bruce W. "Calderón's Comedy and His Serious Sense of

Life." En *Hispanic Studies in Honor of Nicholson B. Adams* 179–93. Chapel Hill: University of North Carolina Press, 1966.

———. "El problema de la responsabilidad en la comedia de capa y espada de Calderón." *Actas del Segundo Congreso Internacional de Hispanistas* 689–94. Nimega, 1967.

Zabaleta, Juan de. *El día de fiesta por la tarde* (1660). Véase Vitse.

Apéndice I[1]

Variantes de las primeras ediciones

LOA

	1681	CH
		La portada de CH reza así: "Loa para la comedia de la Segunda Celestina que se hizo a los años de la Reina nuestra señora, este año de 1675. De D. Agustín de Salazar".
1–8	Interrogaciones.	No son ni exclamaciones ni interrogaciones.
17	Interrogación.	No es interrogación.
21	Interrogación.	No es interrogación.
33		Falta "Representa" la segunda vez.
39	ofrecen	ofrece
48	que es Mariana	de Mariana
57	que siendo yo España, soy	que siendo España, soy
93–4	Con justa razon me llamas, Alemania, porque noten,	Bien, para esso me has llamado Alemania? porque notes,
105		Falta "Cielo" del margen.
112	*Canta Cielo.*	*Cantando el Cielo.*
118	*Canta Tierra.*	*Cantando la Tierra.*
133	culto a la real primavera	culto a augusta primavera
136	*Representa Cielo.*	*Representando.*
137–40		Interrogación.
145–48		Interrogación.
161		Falta "España" del margen.
162		Lo atribuye a "España".

[1] Las erratas que aparecen en las ediciones originales no están corregidas en este apéndice ni se indican siempre por "sic". El propósito del apéndice es proporcionar al lector el estado actual de los textos para que pueda cotejar con facilidad la labor editorial evidente en cada uno.

166		Falta "Las 2".
		que flores, y luz componen:
167		Falta "Alemania" del margen.
170	*Canta el Cielo.*	*Cantando el Cielo.*
174	*Canta la Tierra.*	*Cantando la Tierra.*
178	con voces de olor a la flor [os rendid.	con flores de olor, a la flor [os rendid.
	Sale cantando el Coro de Luces.	*Sale el Coro de Luces, y canta.*
182	*Sale cantando el Coro de Fores.*	*El Coro de Flores.*
185	y entre, amores, albores, [y olores,	y entre amores, favores, [y olores,
186	*Canta Alemania.*	*Cantando Alemania.*
188	tu culto	su culto
190	*Repítese esta copla por toda la Música, y dan principio al sarao.*	*Con esta copla, despuès de haberse cantando[sic], se repitirá otra vez con el sarao.*
194	luciente la flor . . .	ardiente la flor . . .
	Canta Tierra.	*Cantando la Tierra.*
197	y sinceles . . .	y cinceles . . .
198	*Canta Cielo.*	*Cantando el Cielo.*
199–200	Y vuestra amante unión [reverente de olor y de luz . . .	Y vuestra unión luminosa, de flores y luz . . .
202	*Repítase la primera copla por toda la Música, y se dará fin.*	*Repítase la primera copla del sarao, por las cuatro y se dará fin.*

	El encanto es la hermosura	*La segunda Celestina*

JORNADA PRIMERA

		La portadilla reza: "La gran comedia de La segunda Celestina. Fiesta para los años de la Reina nuestra señora, año de 1676. De don Agustin de Salazar. Personas que hablan en ella".
	. . . con escopeta y sombrero con plumas . . .	. . . con plumas y escopeta . . .
8	el plomo y la voz . . .	el plomo y la luz . . .

9	. . . la debe	. . . le debe
45–48		Interrogación.
52	. . mi quinta	. . . esta quinta
64	. . . pese a mi vida	. . . pesia mi vida
72	Señor? . . .	Señor, . . .
74	Muñoz?	Muñoz.
83–85	No es exclamación.	No es exclamación.
91–93		Interrogación.
106–7	¿ha tenido la noticia de que vienes tu enemigo?	de que vienes, la noticia ha tenido tu enemigo?
108	. . . eso me digas	. . . aqueso me digas
110–11	porque a mí nada me implica que lo sepa o no lo sepa.	que a mí que me importaría que lo sepa u no lo sepa?
138	sulcaba	surcaba
145	se llegó a hablarla a la reja	se llegó hablar a la reja
162	advirtiendo	advertiendo [sic]
274	de la . . .	con la . . .
322	son señas . . .	son señal . . .
335	. . . vuelvo	. . . vuelve
353–56		Interrogación.
361	. . . En este caso	. . . Mas por lo menos
368	. . . el que rinda?	. . . que rinda?
395	eso? Ahora . . .	esto hará [sic]? . . .
397–98	Prosigue, que, por hacer tiempo, oiré tus boberías.	Por hacer tiempo, prosigue, que he de oír tus boberías.
401	. . . más se le luce	. . . en ella más luce
454–58		No es exclamación.
466–67		No es interrogación.
479	Al verme . . .	El verme . . .
484	. . . a quien	. . . al que
509	. . . misma	. . . mesma
531	Ah de casa?	Ah de casa.
554	Celestina?	Celestina.
573	. . . aprehendido	. . . aprendido
586	comienza . . .	empieza . . .
597	porque el desdén . . .	porque el rigor . . .
609	sulcábamos . . .	surcábamos . . .
621	a impedir . . .	a dejar . . .
625	mas cree . . .	créeme . . .
661	. . . más, se fue	. . . en fin se fue
680	volver a verte?	volverte a ver?
686	¡Grande . . .	¡Mucho . . .
692	¿Oyes, te acuerdas . . .	¿Oye, acordaráste . . .
699	¿Y la hora?	y la hora . . . [Forma parte del parlamento de

		doña Ana y no es interrogación.]
705–6		Interrogación.
710–11		Interrogación.
713–14		No es interrogación.
724–26	Interrogaciones.	Interrogaciones.
733	Y a la . . .	Y a tu . . .
752	. . . por mí te hablara	. . . me apadrinara
757	asegurado	segurado
769–70		No es interrogación.
771–74		No es interrogación.
814–15	No es exclamación.	No es exclamación.
816	. . . ha sido sólo . . .	. . . sólo ha sido . . .
832–33	Eso de tu vigilancia saber espero.	Eso fío de tu maña que has de saber.
833–34	¿Ni el nombre / siquiera?	¿Ni siquiera / el nombre?
839	Esto	Eso
904	*Dentro ruido de cuchilladas.*	*Ruido de cuchilladas dentro.* Falta "La ventaja".
909	yo	ya
914		Falta *riñendo.*
962	El que anda	Quien anda
964	Señor?	Señor . . . .
996–97		No dice "aparte".
997	iré a hablar	iré hablar
1006	*Salen* DOÑA ANA, DOÑA BEATRIZ, DON LUIS, ANTONIA *y* INES.	*Salen* DOÑA ANA, DOÑA BEATRIZ, INES, ANTONIA *y* DON LUIS, *viejo.*
1010	. . . en el afecto.	. . . en los afectos.
1017	hasta salir de Sevilla.	para ver al asistente.
1043	y te alivies de ese traje,	alíviate de este traje que yo te asistiré luego, y hablaremos mas despacio;
1056		Falta *Vase.*
1094	Falta "que".	
1095		Falta "Que".
1095–96		No es exclamación.
1097		Falta el signo de interrogación.
1097–1000	No es aparte.	No es aparte.
1115–19	No es aparte.	No es aparte.
1116–17	Es interrogación.	No es interrogación ni exclamación.
1118–19		Atribuídas erróneamente a doña Ana.
1120		¡Ay ingrata!
1127–28		Exclamación.

1150–51	A ese duelo presto he de satisfacerte.	Ese duelo presto se satisfará.
1154	¡Cielos, qué es esto que veo!	¡Cielos! ¿Qué es eso que veo?
1155	¿Si es aquésta la que quiere?	¿Es aquésa la que quieres? (No es aparte.)
1157	encanto	engaño
1163–66		No es interrogación.
1191	vaya usted . . .	váyase usted . . .

SEGUNDA JORNADA

1221	se oculta	se alienta
1224	priesa	prisa
1230–31		Interrogación.
1232	No cs aparte.	No es aparte.
1236–40	No es aparte.	No es aparte.
1242–43		Interrogación.
1243	¿Antonia?	Antonia.
1244	¿Señora?	Señora.
1253–54	Esto, sin duda, es que anoche por la reja	Esto es, sin duda, el que anoche por la reja
1253–55		No es aparte.
1262–65		No es aparte.
1266		Se atribuye a doña Beatriz.
1267	¡Prima! ¡Beatriz!	Prima. Beatriz.
1335–36		Forma parte de la exclamación.
1354	. . . encendida Etna	. . . irracional Etna
1358	mal eximirse pudiera	mal eximir se pudiera
1370	purpúrea	púrpura
1385	como mi . . .	como en mi . . .
1421	Esta en mí es obligación	En mí está esta obligación
1425	¿Antonia? ¿Señora?	Atonia. Señora.
1432–33		Interrogación.
1443–44	la docta filosofía a ser damas aprendieran	el saber filosofía el ser damas aprendieran
1471	¿llamaron?	llamaron.
1480	. . . yo a verte venga	. . . a verte yo venga
1508–14	No es interrogación la segunda frase.	No hay signo de interrogación en ninguna.
1525–48		Son interrogaciones.
1564	el . . .	al . . .
1567	Pensarás . . .	¿Pensarás . . . ?

1575–77	Calla, Tacón, si no quieres usar mal de mi paciencia. *TACON* Señor, me ha dado una joya,	No uses mal de mi paciencia, Tacón. *TACON* Me ha dado una joya. (La asonancia se rompe, porque falta un verso.)
1597		Forma parte de la interrogación.
1599	. . . un hombre	. . . a un hombre
1607		No es interrogación.
1614	. . . con promesas	. . . con promesa
1625–26	No es aparte.	No es aparte.
1632	. . . ni vea	. . . o te vea
1645	a arriesgar . . .	arriesgar . . .
1651	querer	el querer
1653–55		Interrogación.
1659	Pensaréis . . .	¿Pensaréis . . . ?
1678		No es interrogación.
1690	Pues yo . . .	Y yo . . .
1695	estéis	estáis
1710	*INES y ANTONIA*	*y ANTONIA, INES*
1716	. . . y se enserpienta.	. . . y enserpienta.
1722	¿Cómo? ¿En mi casa pendencias?	¿Cómo en mi casa pendencias?
1745		No es exclamación.
1763	No es aparte.	No es aparte.
1766–67	No es aparte.	No es aparte.
1769		No hay acotación.
1771	esto por una borracha!	esto por esta borracha!
1779–80	. . . la clamencia?	. . . la clamencia?
1783–84	No son exclamaciones.	No son exclamaciones.
1791	. . . este ladrón.	. . . de ese ladrón.
1808	puedo	quedo [sic]
1813	Pues . . .	¿Pues?
1816–19		No es interrogación.
1835	. . . la pidieren.	. . . le pidieren.
1838–43	¿Celestina? . . . [No es aparte.]	¿Celestina? . . . [No es aparte.]
1842	. . . más prudencia	. . . y más prudencia
1850	sciencia	ciencia
1850–56	No es aparte.	No es aparte.
1868	¡Ay Beatriz, deja que sienta!	¡Ay Beatriz! deja que sienta
1884	¿Yo?	Yo.
1886	. . . ése era	. . . éste era
1887	¿Eso ignoras?	Eso ignoras.
1890–91	No es exclamación.	No es exclamación.
1900	. . . que esto sea	. . . de que sea

1908		llavarte [sic]
1934	¡Qué miro! ¿Es ilusión?	¡Qué miro, es ilusión!
1938	. . . llamó	. . . llama
1941	. . . fingir.	. . . el fingir.
1944	. . . aquel que	. . . a aquel que
1957		Interrogación.
1973	¿Inés? ¿Señora?	¿Inés? Señora.
1975	habiéndola . . .	habiéndole . . .
2005	*DOÑA ANA*	*DON DIEGO*
2024	les negará . . .	las negará . . .
2029	"Silguero"	"Xilguero"
2037	así	ansí
2047–52		Interrogaciones.
2063	. . . ocultarme podía	. . . podía ocultarme
2072	un dolor de otro dolor?	un dolor y otro dolor?
2073–74		Falta.
2074–77		Interrogación.
2079	pronta	prompta
2080–94	Todo es aparte, aunque se nota sólo una vez.	Item.
2080–83		Interrogaciones.
2087	la vida	le [sic] vida
2095	Sabe	Sabe que
2113	señor, puedo . . .	es posible . . .
2115	sciencia	ciencia
2134	Interrogación.	Exclamación.
2140–1		No es aparte.
2150	Eso . . .	Esto . . .
2154	y luego volveré.	y volveré luego.
2155–56		No es exclamación ni interrogación.
2166	que este . . .	porque el . . .
2180–82		No es interrogación.
2183	Celestina.	¿Celestina?
2201	. . . noria	. . . norias
2205	¿Yo me aflijo?	Yo me aflijo.
2207		No es interrogación.
2211	¿Ah caballero escondido?	Ah caballero escondido.
2213	¿Don Diego?	Don Diego.
2219	vuelve	llega
2220	*Escóndese.*	*Va.*
2224	¿Celestina?	Celestina.
2239	sciencia	ciencia
2259	*Va* . . .	*Vase* . . .
2265	¿Ha pasado?	¿Ya ha pasado?

2273	¿Celestina?	Celestina.
2295	ya lo	yo la

JORNADA TERCERA

2310	sciencia	
2304	hayan picado	piquen mucho
2306	es saber hoy . . .	es hoy saber . . .
2316		"a la puerta" falta.
2321	Pues no te tardes.	Pues no tardes. *Escóndese.*
2325	¿Tacón?	¡Tacón!
2337	¿a mí te vienes . . .	¿a mí me vienes . . .
2339–43		Exclamación.
2357–59		No es interrogación.
2382	. . . bellaco	. . . borracho
2383	*Quiere quitarle* . . .	*Quiérele quitar* . . .
2290		*Aparte.*
2392	. . . tacaño	. . . malvado
2403	en que . . .	de que . . .
2420	cielos santos	cielos santos
2430	. . . bien excusado	. . . muy excusado
2456–63	No es aparte.	No es aparte.
2462	. . . a averiguarlo	averiguarlo
2502	este bohios [sic]	*Vase.*
2506		asduo [sic]

Apéndice II

Variantes de las ediciones de la conclusión de Vera Tassis

2611	¿Ah cielos?
2616–24	Exclamación en 1694, H, BAE y TS. En 1681: ¡oh indigna / ley paternal!
2660	sciencia
2713	sciencia
2753–54	Sólo es aparte en BAE y TS.
2766	¿Prima, prima?
2783–88	No se incluye en la interrogación en 1681, 1694 y H.
2802–03	Interrogación en 1681; en 1694 es exclamación.
2856	"Qué sombras" en 1681, 1694 y H.
2881	En lugar de DOÑA BEATRIZ, 1681 pone DON JUAN, error evidente.
2910–11	No es aparte en 1681, 1694 y H.
2923	No es exclamación en 1681, BAE y TS.
2931–34	No se incluye en la exclamación en 1681, 1694 y H.
2952–60	Aparte sólo en TS.
2952–54	Interrogación sólo en BAE y TS.
2970	"Antonia, Inés" en 1681, 1694 y H; es interrogación en BAE y TS.
3030	Pongo la exclamación.
3070	Pongo la exclamación.
3087	No es interrogación en 1681.
3105–06	Sólo es aparte en BAE y TS.
3108–09	Sólo es aparte en BAE y TS.
3133	1681 dice "*a don Juan*".
3155	Exclamación en BAE y TS.
3174	sciencia.
3240	Interrogación en 1681 y 1694.
3308	1681 reza "ponedos," error evidente. Véase el v. 3322.
3379	sciencia.
3422	sciencia.
3434–35	Parte de la interrogación sólo en BAE y TS.
3477	sciencia.
3491	sciencia.
3559–60	Exclamaciones sólo en BAE y TS.

Apéndice III

Variantes de las ediciones de la conclusión de sor Juana

2510–11	No es interrogación.
2520	Pongo la exclamación.
2525–26	No es interrogación.
2559	CH reza "hacia a".
2582	CH dice "y cuando".
2692	difraces [sic]
2699	descurrir
2703	averigar
2757	dzcidme
2889–90	Es exclamación el v. 2889. La pongo en 2890.
2909–10	Exclamaciones en CH, BNM1 y BNM2.
2923	Yo, señora.
2924	"ha hallado" en CH y BNM1; sigo BNM2 aquí.
2945	cierta cosas
2955–60	Pongo el aparte.
2957	quien lo estorba.
2978	. . . en al camino
3014–16	Pongo los apartes.
3036	advitrio
3155–64	Pongo los apartes.
3164	Falta "el".
3171–72	Interrogación; pongo el aparte.
3210–12	"Dios bendito / justicia en mi casa como / es esto?" Añado las exclamaciones.
3214–15	Pongo la interrogación; en CH es exclamación.
3220–21	Pongo la exclamación.
3225–27	No es exclamación en CH y BNM1.
3228	No es exclamación.
3245	entre pisonda
3268	aspacio
3284	este casa . . .
3289–94	No es aparte.
2398	moriré
3305–06	No es interrogación.
3343	finguir

3381	un cartas
3424–28	Pongo el aparte.
3426	alientan
3434	encamiento
3439	trajiese
3455–56	Pongo el aparte.
3459	finguió
2463	No es exclamación.
3498	ser
3508	galeantado (sic)

EL ENCANTO ES LA HERMOSVRA, Y EL HECHIZO SIN HECHIZO,

COMEDIA FAMOSA,

FIESTA AL CVMPLIMIENTO DE AÑOS de la Reyna nueſtra ſeñora Doña Mariana de Auſtria.

DE DON AGVSTIN DE SALAZAR y Torres.

PERSONAS.

Doña Ana.
Doña Beatriz.
Antonia, criada.
Inès, criada.
Celeſtina.
Don Iuan.
Don Diego.
Don Luis, viejo.
Tacon, criado.
Muñoz, criado.

IORNADA PRIMERA.

Sale Doña Beatriz en trage de cazadora, con eſcopeta, y ſombrero con plumas, retirandoſe de Don Iuan, que ſale ſiguiendola, veſtido de camino.

d.Bea. Cauallero, ſi adelante
paſſais, hareis, que mi ira
con la voz deſta eſcopeta
reſponda à vueſtra oſadia.

d.Iuan. Bella Deidad deſtos boſques,
emula hermoſa de Cintia,
que para fieras, y hombres
el plomo, y la voz fulminas:
à quien el Betis la debe
quantas eſtampas floridas
tus negros ojos encienden,
tu blanco pie reſucita;

 per-